# THE OPPOSING SELF

# Also by Lionel Trilling

ESSAYS

Beyond Culture

The Liberal Imagination

A Gathering of Fugitives

BIOGRAPHY

Matthew Arnold

E. M. Forster

NOVEL

The Middle of the Journey

*Edited by Lionel Trilling*

The Portable Matthew Arnold

Selected Letters of John Keats

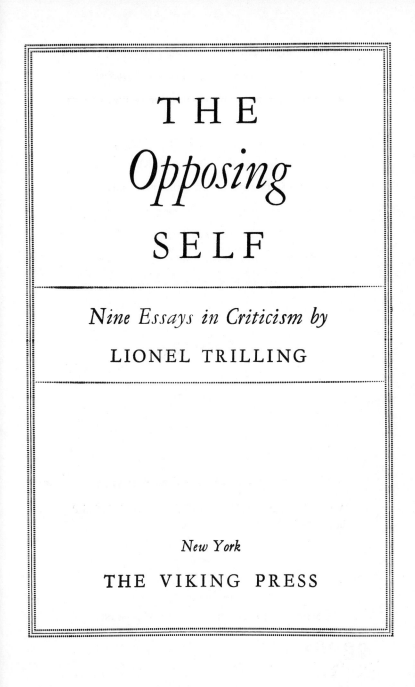

# THE
# *Opposing*
# SELF

*Nine Essays in Criticism by*

LIONEL TRILLING

*New York*

THE VIKING PRESS

COPYRIGHT 1950, 1951, 1952, 1953, 1955 BY LIONEL TRILLING

*The Opposing Self: Nine Essays in Criticism*

ORIGINALLY PUBLISHED BY THE VIKING PRESS, INC., IN 1955


VIKING COMPASS EDITION

ISSUED IN 1959 BY THE VIKING PRESS, INC.

625 MADISON AVENUE, NEW YORK, N.Y. 10022

DISTRIBUTED IN CANADA BY

THE MACMILLAN COMPANY OF CANADA LIMITED

SECOND PRINTING MARCH 1968

Library of Congress catalog card number: 55-5871

A record of earlier publication of these essays is included
in the Author's Note, pages 231-32.

PRINTED IN THE U.S.A. BY THE COLONIAL PRESS INC.

*To James and Elsa Grossman*

# Contents

Preface                                                        ix

The Poet as Hero: Keats in His Letters                          3

Little Dorrit                                                   50

Anna Karenina                                                   66

William Dean Howells and the Roots of Modern Taste             76

The Bostonians                                                 104

Wordsworth and the Rabbis                                      118

George Orwell and the Politics of Truth                        151

Flaubert's Last Testament                                      173

Mansfield Park                                                 206

# Preface

M o s t of these essays were written as introductions to books, and all of them were written for occasions which were not of my own devising. The occasions were quite discrete from one another, the subjects are in some ways diverse, and I wrote the essays with no thought of achieving an interconnection among them. In each case my intention was only to serve the given subject, to say what makes a particular book or author interesting and valuable to us. Yet inevitably an interconnection among the essays does exist—apart, I mean, from whatever coherence is to be found in their writer's notions of what constitutes the interesting and the valuable, of what constitutes "us." The essays deal with episodes of the literature of the last century and a half, and they all, in one way or another, take account of the idea that preoccupies this literature and is central to it, and makes its principle and its unity—the idea of the self.

There have always been selves, or at least ever since the oracle at Delphi began to advise every man to know his own. And whoever has read any European history at all knows that the self emerges (as the historians say) at pretty frequent intervals. Yet the self that makes itself manifest at the end of the eighteenth century is different in kind, and in effect, from any self that had ever before emerged. It is different in several notable respects, but there is one distinguishing characteristic which seems to me pre-eminently important: its intense and adverse imagination of the culture in which it has its being.

I speak of the relation of the self to *culture* rather than to *society* because there is a useful ambiguity which attends the meaning of the word culture. It is the word by which we refer not only to a people's achieved works of intellect and imagination but also to its mere assumptions and unformulated valuations, to its habits, its manners, and its superstitions. The modern self is characterized by certain powers of indignant perception which, turned upon this unconscious portion of culture, have made it accessible to conscious thought.

One of the essays of this book, that on Dickens' *Little Dorrit,* remarks on the frequency with which the image of the prison appears in the imaginative works of the nineteenth century; and this, as the essay goes on to say, seems natural enough when we remember that the new age was signalized by the fall of a very famous prison, the Bastille. The attack on the Bastille was an attack on the gross injustices and irrationalities of the social system. These gross injustices and irrationalities were not wiped out in 1789, nor were they forgotten in the years that followed. But as soon as the Bastille had fallen, the image of the prison came to represent something more than the gross injustices and irrationalities. Men began to recognize the existence of prisons that were not built of stone, nor even of social restrictions and economic disabilities. They learned to see that they might be immured not only by the overt force of society but by a coercion in some ways more frightful because it involved their own acquiescence. The newly conceived coercive force required of each prisoner that he sign his own *lettre de cachet,* for it had established its prisons in the family life, in the professions, in the image of respectability, in the ideas of faith and duty, in (so the poets said) the very language itself. The modern self, like Little Dorrit, was born in a prison. It assumed its nature and fate the moment it perceived, named, and denounced its oppressor.

And by this act it brought into being not only itself but also the idea of culture as a living thing with a fate of its own, with the possibility, and the necessity, of its own redemption.

The best account of the strange, bitter, dramatic relation between the modern self and the modern culture is that which Hegel gives in the fourth part of his *Philosophy of History*. Few people nowadays have a good word for Hegel, and I—who am not, I had better say, a Hegelian—have no doubt that he is in everybody's bad books for the right reasons. But if we think of Hegel not in his political aspect but simply as an observer and describer of the developing culture of our time, we cannot but recognize his power. It was he who first spoke of the "alienation" which the modern self contrives as a means for the fulfillment of its destiny, and of the pain which the self incurs because of this device of self-realization. And it was he who, speaking of the principle of culture, and of course speaking in its defense, referred to it as the *terrible* principle of culture.

Hegel understood in a remarkable way what he believed to be a new phenomenon of culture, a kind of cultural mutation. This is the bringing into play in the moral life of a new category of judgment, the category of quality. Not merely the deed itself, he said, is now submitted to judgment, but also the personal quality of the doer of the deed. It has become not merely a question of whether the action conforms to the appropriate principle or maxim of morality, but also of the manner in which it is performed, of what it implies about the entire nature, the *being,* of the agent. This is what Hegel had in mind when he instituted his elaborate distinction between "character" and "personality," the latter term having reference to what we might call the manner and style of the moral action.

His perception of this new mode of judgment Hegel in part derived from his reading of the new literature of his day, and it was one of the things that led to his giving to art an importance quite without precedent in moral philosophy. For Hegel, art is the activity of man in which spirit expresses itself not only as utility, not only according to law, but as grace, as transcendence, as manner and style. He brought together the moral and the aesthetic judgment. He did this not in the old way of making morality the criterion of the aesthetic: on the contrary, he made the aesthetic the criterion of the moral.

Much the same thing was done in a simpler way by a literary critic who never, I believe, read Hegel. Matthew Arnold said of literature that it was a criticism of life. No doubt there is extravagance in the statement. Literature has perhaps not always been, and is not in its essence, a criticism of life. But as the statement refers to the literature of the modern period, it is strikingly accurate. It lost a good deal of its authority with us after T. S. Eliot's adverse comment on it in the preface to the second edition of *The Sacred Wood*. Arnold framed his famous sentence in two versions, sometimes with "literature," sometimes with "poetry" as its subject, and of Arnold's having called poetry a criticism of life Mr. Eliot observed that "no phrase can sound more frigid to anyone who has felt the full surprise and elevation of a new experience of poetry." This may be true, and perhaps Arnold's phrase needed to be roughly handled because it seemed to license a dull way of reading poetry. But if now, after the passage of a good many years, we look again at the words which Mr. Eliot used to discredit Arnold's phrase, we see that they actually serve to explicate and to justify it. They tell us precisely in what way

Arnold thought that poetry was a criticism of life. *Surprise and elevation:* set the words over against Arnold's sense of our life in culture, against his sense of modern culture as a kind of prison (so he called it) and we know very well what Arnold meant. The "frigidity" of his phrase could not have been wholly lost on Arnold himself. When he said that poetry was criticism—which in any ordinary meaning it so obviously isn't—he meant to shock us. He meant to say that in our modern situation the surprise and elevation of poetry can serve to bring to mind some notion of what is the right condition of the self—in general, and not merely when it is having the experience of poetry. He was proposing to us the idea that our culture is hostile to surprise and elevation, and to the freedom of the self which they imply.

He meant, in short, that poetry is a criticism of life in the same way that the Scholar Gipsy was a criticism of the life of an inspector of elementary schools. Our habits of feeling have changed since the time when Arnold's poem had a special place in the world's affection—we are no longer quite suited by the large sadness with which it speaks of the loss of peace and joy. And yet there isn't, I think, a more comprehensive and comprehensible delineation of the modern self in its relation to the culture than that which Arnold makes in this elegy for his own youth. We are all likely to be aware of the Arnold of duty, the Arnold who tried to enforce upon his readers the importance of morality, and the pain and suffering that the moral life entails. But in "The Scholar Gipsy" we have an Arnold who represents duty as a grim second-best, who speaks of the "patience" which the life in culture requires as "too-near neighbor to despair." It is the despair of those who, having committed themselves to culture, have surrendered the life of surprise and elevation, of impulse, pleasure, and imagination. The Scholar Gipsy *is* poetry —he *is* imagination, impulse, and pleasure: he is what virtually every writer of the modern period conceives, the experience of art projected into the actuality and totality of life as the ideal form of the moral life. His existence is intended to disturb us and make us dissatisfied with our habitual life in culture, whose nature his existence defines.

We recognize him as one with the free-ranging boys of Wordsworth's poems, upon whom the shades of the prison house are inevitably to fall, upon whom custom, or culture, is to lie "like a weight,/ Heavy as frost, and deep almost as life." He has a clear affinity across the Atlantic with the boy who started from Paumanok, "the boy ecstatic" whose intensity of selfhood was to serve him as "hardest basic fact, and only entrance to all facts." For us of the immediate present he has his avatar in the legendary figure of Yeats. There is perhaps not much of Arnold's poetry that, at the present time, can be related to Yeats's, and we are likely to be startled when we come on the record of a little pilgrimage which Yeats undertook in the year in which he published his first volume of poems—on a visit to Oxford, as he says in a letter of 1889, he spent a long day "going to the places in Matthew Arnold's poems—the ford in the 'Scholar Gipsy' being the furthest away and the most interesting." The poem, of course, is a prefiguration of Yeats's whole career; it gives us the terms of his long quarrel with the culture, which, more than anything else, made his passion and his selfhood. Such quarrels with the culture we recognize as the necessity not only of the self but of culture.

I have dealt in these essays with more novelists than poets, but of course the novelists in their own way of particularity and circumstantiality are no less committed than the poets to the modern imagination of autonomy and delight, of surprise and elevation, of selves conceived in opposition to the general culture. This imagination makes, I believe, a new idea in the world. It is an idea in the world, not in literature alone. If these essays have a unity, it is because they take notice of this idea, and of its vicissitudes, modulations, and negations.

Most of the essays have been revised since their first publication, but none has been radically revised. I am grateful to the publishers and editors who have permitted me to reprint them here.

# THE OPPOSING SELF

# The Poet as Hero:
# Keats in His Letters

## [ 1 ]

IN THE history of literature the letters of John Keats are unique. All personal letters are interesting; the letters of great men naturally have an especial attraction; and among the letters of great men those of the great creative artists are likely to be the most intimate, the liveliest, and the fullest of wisdom. Yet even among the great artists Keats is perhaps the only one whose letters have an interest which is virtually equal to that of their writer's canon of created work. No other letters, for example, have ever been the occasion of such a warning as F. R. Leavis felt it necessary to give a few years ago. Dr. Leavis said that in thinking about Keats as a poet we must be sure to understand that the important documents are his poems, not his letters. No one will wish to dispute the point with Dr. Leavis. When we think about Keats as a poet, his letters are of course illuminating and suggestive, yet in relation to Keats as a poet they are not primary but secondary; they are no more than illuminating and suggestive. The fact is, however, that because of the letters it is impossible to think of Keats only as a poet—inevitably we think

3

of him as something even more interesting than a poet, we think of him as a man, and as a certain kind of man, a hero.

To be sure, no hero, no man who fully engages our attention, is ever a man in the abstract but is always marked and distinguished by some particular role. We know him as he is a lover, a husband, a father, a son, and it is so much the better if we also know him through his profession, as, say, a king, or a soldier, or a poet. "Othello's *occupation*'s gone!"—the famous pathos of the cry reminds us that in tragic story men are first vulnerable not in their abstract humanity but in the particular commitments of their lives. And so we cannot think of Keats as a man without thinking of him in his occupation of poet. At the same time, when once we have read his letters, we cannot help knowing that his being a poet was his chosen way of being a man.

The charm of Keats's letters is inexhaustible, and we can scarcely hope to define it wholly or to name all its elements. Yet we can be sure that some part of its effect comes from Keats's conscious desire to live life in the heroic mode. In a young man this is always most winning. Keats was situated in a small way of life, that of the respectable, liberal, intellectual middle part of the middle class; his field of action was limited to the small continuous duties of the family; his deportment was marked by quietness and modesty, at times by a sort of diffident neutrality. He nevertheless at every moment took life in the largest possible way and seems never to have been without the sense that to be, or to become, a man was an adventurous problem. The phrase in his letters that everyone knows, "life is a vale of soul-making," is his summing up of that sense, which, once we have become aware of its existence in him, we understand to have dominated his mind. He believed that life was given for him to find the right use of it, that it was a kind of continuous magical confrontation requiring to be met with the right answer. He believed that this answer was to be derived from intuition, courage, and the accumulation of experience. It was not, of course, to be a formula of any kind, not a piece of rationality, but rather a way of being and of acting. And yet it could in part be derived from taking thought, and it could be put, if not into a formula, then at least into many formulations. Keats was nothing if not a man of ideas.

His way of conceiving of life is characteristic of the spirited young man of high gifts—except that it is also characteristic of the very great older men whom the young men of spirit and gifts are most likely to take seriously. Its charm in Keats is the greater because its span is so short and so dramatically concise. Keats is twenty when the letters begin, and he is twenty-six when they end. But he was strikingly precocious—I am inclined to think even more precocious in his knowledge of the world than in poetry. He was one of that class of geniuses who early learn to trust themselves in an essential way, whatever moments of doubt they may have. He was remarkably lucky, or wise, in finding a circle of friends who believed in his powers before he had given much evidence of their existence beyond the communicated sense of his heroic vision, and these friends expected him to speak out. He therefore at a very early age passed beyond all self-conscious hesitation about looking deep into life and himself, about propounding the great questions and attempting the great answers, and about freely telling his thoughts. And so we have the first of the vital contradictions which make the fascination of Keats's mind—we have the wisdom of maturity arising from the preoccupations of youth. This wisdom is the proud, bitter, and joyful acceptance of tragic life which we associate pre-eminently with Shakespeare. It explains the force, as the sense of adventure explains the charm, of Keats's letters.

## [ 2 ]

Bernard Shaw does not seem the likeliest person to help us toward an understanding of Keats as a man, and indeed the little essay on Keats which he once contributed to a memorial volume is for the most part perfunctory. Yet in the course of this essay Shaw speaks at some length of a quality of Keats which, at least for our time, may well be the one which we ought to recognize before any other. This quality is what Shaw calls Keats's *geniality*.

The word is not in good repute nowadays. It is seldom used in common speech, and when it is used at all it is likely to be associated with men of middle age or of hale old age—to many readers it will imply precisely what is not young and fervent, and it will have overtones of a mediocre good will that verges upon a vulgar lack of personal discriminativeness. It will suggest anything but the dedication and impatient creative energy of a young poet. But the word was not always limited by these connotations. It was not thus limited in Keats's own time. It was then a word clearly applicable to a young man: Wordsworth speaks of "the genial sense of youth." And it was precisely applicable to the idea of creativeness: when Coleridge wants to express the idea that he has lost his creative powers, he says that his "genial spirits fail," and one sense of the word that he here intends is that which derives from *genius*.[1]

---

[1] For the Romantic poets the English word was no doubt reinforced by the German word, although *genial* in German had meanings that would not have recommended it to Wordsworth and Coleridge—when G. H. Lewes, in his *Life of Goethe,* describes the wild life of the young men of Weimar and their free sexuality, he says that their actions were understood and forgiven as being typical of the *genial* period and adds in a footnote: "It is difficult to find an English word to express the German *genial,* which means pertaining to genius. The genial period was the period when every extravagance was excused on the plea of genius." Even Goethe's bad spelling, as George Eliot notes in one of her letters from Germany, was spoken of as *genial*.

The word is rich in other high meanings that will be worth noting in relation to Keats. But it will not do for us to ignore the single rather commonplace meaning which we now assign to it, the meaning of simple good-humoredness and sociability. Our notions about "the" poetic temperament being what they are, the sensitive reader is likely to shrink from Shaw's description of Keats as "not only a poet, but a merry soul, a jolly fellow, who could not only carry his splendid burthen of genius, but swing it around, toss it up and catch it again, and whistle a tune as he strode along." This is certainly not the way to describe Keats, yet it is righter than the impulse to consider this description of a poet somehow blasphemous. Nowadays our theory of poetic creation holds that the poet derives his power from some mutilation he has suffered. We take it for granted that he writes out of a darkness of the spirit or not at all. But this was not the belief of the great poets of Keats's own time, and it was not Keats's belief. Wordsworth and Coleridge thought that poetry depended upon a condition of positive health in the poet, a more than usual well-being. Keats himself seems to have had no analogous theory of the right circumstance for creation, but it is clear that for him the writing of poetry was first a regular work, his occupation, which he practiced with sober diligence, and then a great joy. For several obvious reasons, he was much concerned with health; the word occurs very frequently in his poems, and he hated ill health, whether physical or mental. Like any person, he had times of depression; and like any person of intellect, he might give expression to these moods in gloomy generalizations. Like any literary person, he had times when he seemed to feel nothing at all, in which he was without impulse and almost without personality. But he set no store by his dark hours. He was sure that negation was not of his essence, and that it must pass for him to be himself again.

He writes to his brother George of a method he had devised for dealing with depression: "Whenever I find myself growing vapourish, I rouse myself, wash and put on a clean shirt, brush my hair and clothes, tie my shoestrings neatly, and in fact adonize as I were going out—then all clean and comfortable I sit down to write. This I find the greatest relief."

"In fact adonize as I were going out"—how much this tells us about Keats. He never, he said, wrote a line with public intention, and yet when he wishes to summon up his most private faculties and bring them to high pitch, he does so by preparing himself as if for company. He had a passion for friendship and society. It is a statement that needs modification, but as at first we see him he has not the least impulse to hold himself aloof from the common pleasures of men—the community of pleasure, the generality of geniality, are an important part of his daily life. And for quite a long time he believed that the development of his mind was scarcely less communal than were his pleasures. He felt that his friends, most of whom were older than he, had much to give him and were liberal in their giving. And very likely he was right. If we suppose that Keats's own large generosity perhaps estimated at too high a rate what they did give, we must also suppose that his generosity had the actual effect of calling forth a respondent generosity from them.

In his lively sense of social connection Keats was sharing a quality of his time: the life of art and intellect was then more genial than it is now. Men of the same artistic craft, or practitioners of different crafts who stood in the same relation to the public and to the established traditions, thought it becoming in them to admire and defend each other and to be often in each other's company for professional discussion, or merely for puns and jokes. Quarrels and jealousies of course developed, as we find them developing in Keats's circle, but the impulse was stronger than it is now toward the coterie, the *cénacle,* the little group that understood the purposes and legitimate ambitions of each of its members. The Romanticists revived the ideal of friendship, of comradeship in arms, which had been so commanding both in the Middle Ages and in the Renaissance. It was an ideal appropriate to a time that necessarily thought of new art as a political act, almost as a conspiracy.

To this strong tendency of sociability and friendship Keats happily contributed, and the quality of his letters is in part to be explained by it. Not all of Keats's friends were artists, but all lived in the ambiance of the ideals of art and intellect, which, for young men, is likely to have the coloring of bohemianism. And the delicacy of feeling and the cogency of observation of Keats's letters would scarcely have appeared had not Keats been able carelessly to entrust his thoughts to his friends—and not his second thoughts but his first. We owe the wonderful, misspelled immediacy of the letters not only to confidence between friend and friend but also to the free manners of the group, which are of a piece with the generality of the masculine manners of the time. Men then, it would seem, made more occasions for exclusively masculine social diversion, and their habits were livelier than now. The set that Keats consorted with was by no means unmannerly. In the nature of the case, to be sure, there could be no emphasis on "family," and the claims of some of its members to be considered gentlemen might be disallowed by the old, almost technical definition of that rank. Nevertheless gentility was of its essence; and Keats himself, the grandson of a livery-stable keeper, the son of a former ostler and of a mother whose behavior and status became more than questionable, put a high value upon manners, and his own were, I think, exquisite. Yet Keats insisted on manners that were comfortable, and he happily tolerated those that were rowdy. Out of his admiration of Wordsworth the poet, he had every wish to excuse the failings of the man, but toward Wordsworth's stiffness in society no one could have been more severe than he. And with what enjoyment he writes of the raffish dinner of January 1818, with its extreme and elaborate sexual joking and its larking about chamber-pots. Keats would not have understood the ideal of delicacy of the later nineteenth century, which, so far as it manifested itself in the society of men, would have seemed to him strange and foolish.[2] The Regency manners did not in the least offend him, they suited him very well, and they account in some part for the directness and vigor of his correspondence. He and his friends attended bear-baitings and were fond of the raffish world of the prize ring. Keats, among whose books was a volume called *Fencing Familiarized,* was an excellent boxer, and he did not, we know, hesitate to engage a heavier opponent in earnest and with bare fists; he did very well on this occasion. For all his passion for what he called "abstractions," for all the ideality of his poetry, Keats loved the actuality of life; its coarseness and commonness delighted him. "Wonders are no wonders to me," he wrote in November 1819. "I am more at home amongst Men and Women. I would rather read Chaucer than Ariosto." His sense of actuality was quick and racy and in the line of the English poetic humorists from Chaucer and Skelton to Burns. "Dawlish Fair" and "Modern Love" are no doubt to be called exceptional among Keats's poems, but they are of the very stuff of his temperament as the letters show it.

In speaking of Keats's social geniality we shall not be accurate if we do not recognize that there was an element of his personal-

---

[2] It did not manifest itself quite so thoroughly as we have come to believe—the unpublished portions of Samuel Butler's notebooks give an enlightening account of the actual habits and conversation of the gentlemen of his period. But no doubt Butler's having been at such pains to record the facts suggests what the dominant behavior was.

ity which acted to check it. His illness, of course, embittered him, separating him, as he grew more certain of his death, from those who still had the prospect of life, making him suspicious and jealous. But even before his illness he had already begun to withdraw from sociability. It was perhaps to be expected. Early in his career he had expressed to Bailey his confidence in his understanding of the springs of human action. It was an understanding which he was willing to say was exceptional. "As soon as I had known Haydon three days I had got enough of his character not to have been surprised at such a letter as he has hurt you with." "Before I felt interested in either Reynolds or Haydon—I was well read in their faults." But with the quick understanding of human failing goes a most profound tolerance: "—Men should bear with each other—there lives not the Man who may not be cut up, aye hashed to pieces on his weakest side." And the sure way of friendship, he says, "is first to know a man's faults, and then be passive—if after that he insensibly draws you toward him then you have no Power to break the link."

The tolerance was as affectionate as the understanding was undeceived, yet an understanding so undeceived could not allow Keats's social life to be a simple one. There came a time when he found that he was embarrassing himself and annoying his friends by replying not to their spoken remarks but to their unspoken intentions.

Modest as he was in all his relations, inclined as he was to a quiet generosity of admiration, Keats had nevertheless a lively and jealous pride. He early withdrew from Leigh Hunt because Hunt spoke patronizingly of his poetry. He was always cool to Shelley, suspecting condescension. He began to see that one reason for his being liked was his retiring quietness, a certain courteous withdrawal from social competitiveness which he

practiced. "Think of my Pleasure in Solitude," he writes, "in
comparison of my commerce with the world—there I am a
child—there they do not know me, not even my most intimate
acquaintance—I give into their feelings as though I were re-
fraining from irritating a little child—Some think me middling,
others silly, others foolish—everyone thinks he sees my weak
side against my will, when in truth it is with my will—I am
content to be thought all this because I have in my own breast
so great a resource. This is one reason why they like me so;
because they can all show to great advantage in a room, and
eclipse from a certain tact one who is reckoned a good Poet—."
And again: ". . . I suffer greatly by going into parties where
from the rules of society and a natural pride I am obliged to
smother my Spirit and look like an Idiot—because I feel that
my impulses given way to would too much amaze them—I live
under an everlasting restraint—never relieved except when I
am composing— So I will write away."

Keats's separateness must indeed be mentioned but it must
not be exaggerated. In part it was but what we all feel. Keats
might say that he admired human nature and disliked men, but
everybody says that, or says its converse, or both. We are all
naturally not satisfied by the society around us. It never really
lends itself to our purposes and expectations. Of Keats this was
especially true. For him there was perhaps only one man, Shakespeare, who ever satisfied his notion of what men might be. But
his separateness must also be understood as a normal aspect of
his genius. It came to him in the natural course of his growing
awareness of his power and identity, of the work there was for
him to do and the destiny he must fulfill. The remarkable thing
is not that he was separate, that he held the social world at some
small distance by means of his knowledge of it, but rather that
he was not more apart. His knowledge of men checked and

controlled and dignified, but never limited, his geniality. Up to the end it expresses itself in his letters like an animal potency, strangely manifesting itself even when, in the bitterness of approaching death, he experiences spasms of hatred of the friends he loved.

## [ 3 ]

When we think about Keats's social geniality, it is easy and natural for us to suppose that it is the development of his relation to his family. If Keats is genial, he is so in one of the elementary meanings of the word: he is of the *gens,* the family, and, by extension, the tribe, ultimately the nation. "I like, I love England," he said. Solitary as he might be in his mind, he was never a man for physical solitude. Company gave him pleasure. He lived but little alone. He could even compose in the same room with someone else. He liked, we may say, to reconstitute the family situation.

In the nineteenth century it came increasingly to be believed that alienation from the family was indispensable to the poet's growth, and nowadays our mythology of the poetic personality takes this for granted. But Keats would not have understood what we so easily assume. In him family feeling was enormously strong and perfectly direct. Or at least this is true of his feelings toward his brothers and sister. Of what he felt for his deceased parents we can speak only speculatively. But his affection for the brothers and sister is a definitive part of his character and legend. He devoted his life to the care of young Tom in the long last months of the boy's tuberculosis. His letters to George in America are those in which he most opened his heart and mind. To his sister Fanny he was unremitting in tenderness, and, so far as the Abbeys would permit, in solicitude; it was her image, together with that of the other Fanny, that haunted him on the Italian voyage. His familial feeling amounted to what he called a passion.

There is yet another aspect of Keats's geniality of which we must take account. This is his geniality toward himself. We cannot understand Keats's mind without a very full awareness of what powers of enjoyment he had and of how freely he licensed these powers. The pleasure of the senses was for him not merely desirable—it was the very ground of life. It was, moreover, the ground of thought. More than any other poet—more, really, than Shelley—Keats is Platonic, but his Platonism is not doctrinal or systematic: it was by the natural impulse of his temperament that his mind moved up the ladder of love which Plato expounds in *The Symposium,* beginning with the love of things and moving toward the love of ideas, with existences and moving toward essences, with appetites and moving toward immortal longings. But the movement is of a special kind, perhaps of a kind that the orthodox interpretation of Plato cannot approve. For it is not, so to speak, a biographical movement—Keats does not, as he develops, "advance" from a preoccupation with sense to a preoccupation with intellect. Rather it is his characteristic mode of thought all through his life to begin with sense and to move thence to what he calls "abstraction," but never to leave sense behind. Sense cannot be left behind, for of itself it generates the idea and remains continuous with it. And the moral and speculative intensity with which Keats's poems and letters are charged has its unique grace and illumination because it goes along with, and grows out of, and conditions, but does not deny, the full autonomy of sense.

But it is not enough to speak of Keats's loyalty to sense, nor is it even enough to speak of his loyalty to the pleasures of the senses. *Sense* and *pleasures of the senses* may apply as well to

Wordsworth as to Keats. We must make no mistake about it: when it comes to sense and pleasure, Keats is Wordsworth's disciple, and the great difference between the ways in which they understood the two words must not blind us to the similarities. Here, however, we are concerned with the significant difference. Our language distinguishes between the sensory, the sensuous, and the sensual. The first word is neutral as regards pleasure, the second connotes pleasure of varying degrees and kinds but is yet distinguished from the last, which suggests pleasure that is intense, appetitive, material, and which usually carries a strong pejorative overtone and almost always an implication of sexuality. For Wordsworth the pleasures of the senses are the clear sign of rightness of life, but virtually the only two sense-faculties of which he takes account are seeing and hearing, and, at that, the seeing and hearing of only a few kinds of things; and the matter of the senses' experience passes very quickly into what Wordsworth calls the "purer mind" and has been but minimally sensuous, let alone sensual. For Keats, however, there was no distinction of prestige among the senses, and to him the sensory, the sensuous, and the sensual were all one. Wordsworth would have happily concurred in the sentiment which Keats expresses when, writing to his friend Brown, he speaks of "the pleasures which it was your duty to procure," for Wordsworth had identified the "native and naked dignity of man" with the "grand elementary principle of pleasure, by which he knows, and feels, and lives, and moves." But Wordsworth would have withdrawn hastily when Keats urges the newly married Reynolds to "gorge the honey of life." Particularly because of the sexual context, but not because of that alone, he would have been dismayed by the appetitive image and the frankness of appetite amounting to greed.

But it is, of course, exactly the appetitive image and the frankness of his appetite that we cannot dispense with in our understanding of Keats. Eating and the delicacies of taste are basic and definitive in his experience and in his poetry. The story of his putting cayenne pepper on his tongue in order to feel the more intensely the pleasure of a draft of cold claret is apocryphal. Yet it is significant that Haydon, who told the story, was sufficiently aware of Keats's disposition to have invented it. It does not, after all, go beyond Keats's own account of his pleasure in the nectarine. "Talking of pleasure," he writes to Dilke, "this moment I was writing with one hand, and with the other holding to my mouth a Nectarine—good God how fine. It went down soft, slushy, oozy—all its delicious embonpoint melted down my throat like a beatified Strawberry."

We are ambivalent in our conception of the moral status of eating and drinking. On the one hand ingestion supplies the imagery of our largest and most intense experiences: we speak of the wine of life and the cup of life; we speak also of its dregs and lees, and sorrow is also something to be drunk from a cup; shame and defeat are wormwood and gall; divine providence is manna or milk and honey; we hunger and thirst for righteousness; we starve for love; lovers devour each other with their eyes; and scarcely a mother has not exclaimed that oh, she could eat her baby up; bread and salt are the symbols of peace and loyalty, bread and wine the stuff of the most solemn acts of religion. On the other hand, however, while we may represent all of significant life by the tropes of eating and drinking, we do so with great circumspection. Our use of the ingestive imagery is rapid and sparse, never developed; we feel it unbecoming to dwell upon what we permit ourselves to refer to.[3]

[3] The phrase "manna from heaven" is a common one, but no one ever says "quail from heaven," even though the quail were just as important as the manna in the diet which was divinely provided for the Children of Israel in the wilderness; manna, we might say, was but the divine dessert. Yet because manna was evanescent and is

But with Keats the ingestive imagery is pervasive and extreme. He is possibly unique among poets in the extensiveness of his reference to eating and drinking and to its pleasurable or distasteful sensations. To some readers this is likely to be alienating, and indeed even a staunch admirer might well become restive under, for example, Keats's excessive reliance on the word "dainties" to suggest all pleasures, even the pleasures of literature. It is surely possible to understand what led Yeats to speak of Keats as a boy with his face pressed to the window of a sweetshop. The mild and not unsympathetic derogation of Yeats's image suggests something of the reason for the negative part of our ambivalence toward eating and drinking. The ingestive appetite is the most primitive of our appetites, the sole appetite of our infant state, and a preoccupation with it, an excessive emphasis upon it, is felt—and not without some reason—to imply the passivity and self-reference of the infantile condition. No doubt that is why Ciacco, the glutton of the *Inferno,* although not accounted the worst sinner in hell, is, as it were, the most dehumanized—not the most *inhuman* as we habitually use that word, but the most disgusting; he has not even grown into the adult activity which might lead to aggressive wickedness, but sits passive under the fall of stinking snow: his is the peculiar horribleness of a grown man who is still an infant. And religious satirists of modern life, such as Aldous Huxley, T. S. Eliot, or Graham Greene, when they wish to make a character represent the malign infantilism of our contemporary materialist culture, ascribe to him an undue and detailed interest in eating. In this connection it is worth noting that we consent to be delighted by the description of great feasts as in

---

not to be identified with any known edible thing, it has come to serve as a metaphor for miraculous sustenance and spiritual comfort; the quail, being all too grossly actual, have been quite forgotten!

Homer, Rabelais, and Dickens; the communal aspect of the eating implies "maturity" and allays our fears of infantile narcissism. This is especially true if the food is plain and hearty and does not suggest cosseting, and if the appetites match it in this respect, for largeness of appetite has a moral sanction which fineness of appetite can never have.

But Keats did not share our culture's fear of the temptation to the passive self-reference of infancy. He did not repress the infantile wish; he confronted it, recognized it, and delighted in it. Food—and what for the infant usually goes with food, a cozy warmth—made for him the form, the elementary idea, of felicity. He did not fear the seduction of the wish for felicity, because, it would seem, he was assured that the tendency of his being was not that of regression but that of growth. The knowledge of felicity was his first experience—he made it the ground of all experience, the foundation of his quest for truth. Thus, for Keats, the luxury of food is connected with, and in a sense gives place to the luxury of sexuality. The best known example of this is the table spread with "dainties" beside Madeline's bed in "The Eve of St. Agnes." And in that famous scene the whole paraphernalia of luxurious felicity, the invoked warmth of the south, the bland and delicate food, the privacy of the bed, and the voluptuousness of the sexual encounter, are made to glow into an island of bliss with the ultimate dramatic purpose of making fully apparent the cold surrounding darkness; it is the moment of life in the infinitude of not-being. As an image of man's life it has the force of the Venerable Bede's apologue of the sparrow that flew out of the night of winter storm through the warmth and light of the king's ale-hall and out again into darkness. Keats's capacity for pleasure implies his capacity for the apprehension of tragic reality.

It also serves his capacity for what he called *abstraction*. I have said that he was the most Platonic of poets. Ideas, abstractions, were his life. He lived to perceive ultimate things, essences. This is what appetite, or love, was always coming to mean for him. Plato said that Love is the child of Abundance and Want, and for Keats it was just that. In one of the most remarkable passages of his letters he says that the heart "is the teat from which the mind or intelligence sucks identity." The first appetite prefigures the last; the first ingestive image is constant for this man who, in his last sonnet, speaks of "the palate of my mind," and who images the totality of life by the single grape which is burst against "the palate fine."

## [ 4 ]

What I have called Keats's geniality toward himself, his bold acceptance of his primitive appetite and his having kept open a line of communication with it, had its decisive effect upon the nature of his creative intelligence. It had an effect no less decisive upon his moral character.

In speaking of Keats's appetitive inclination, we cannot ignore the element of heredity. There has been ascribed to his mother's father an extravagant concern with food—Mr. Jennings was said to have been so extreme in his love of eating that his wife and family spent four days in the week preparing for the Sunday dinner. His daughter, Keats's mother, was said to have resembled him in this gormandizing character, "but she was more remarkably the Slave of other Appetites attributable probably to this for their exciting Cause." The witness, to be sure, is Mr. Abbey, Keats's guardian, who was no doubt narrow in his views, and admirers of Keats naturally dislike him and allow him little credit or credence. Yet it was to the admirable John Taylor, Keats's publisher and loyal friend, that Abbey told his story;

Taylor was an intelligent man and he must have known in some detail of the dealings of Abbey with the Keats children, yet Taylor speaks of Abbey as "kind hearted" and "good," and did not, as we are inclined to do, dismiss his testimony out of a pious partisanship but, on the contrary, thought him a man worthy of belief. And although Abbey may well have been exaggerating, he was not necessarily making it up out of whole cloth when he said that the young Frances Jennings was so ardent in her passions that it was dangerous to be alone with her, and that at an early age she had told him that she must have and would have a husband. We make what discount we will for Mr. Abbey's susceptibility and for his narrowness of view, even for his spite, and still we cannot but suppose that Frances was of a lively and straightforward sexual temperament. Abbey said that she was a pretty little woman (but Cowden Clark says she was tall) with regular features, although her mouth was too wide. He remembered that she troubled a certain shopkeeper on rainy days because she held her skirts too high in crossing the street, showing "uncommonly handsome legs." [4]

Whether or not Frances Keats was, in the conventional sense, a good woman and a good mother is a hard judgment to make. The piety of biographers inclines to say that she was, or at least that she was not bad, and explains her second marriage three months after the death of her husband as a necessary practical step to maintain the livery stable, and dismisses as a mere canard Abbey's story that after leaving Rawlings, the unendurable second husband, she formed a liaison with a Jew named Abraham

[4] Abbey's account of Mrs. Keats is reported in a letter of John Taylor as given in *The Keats Circle,* edited by Hyder Edward Rollins (Cambridge: Harvard University Press, 1948). The testimony of George Keats and of Reynolds, cited in the following pages, is from the same source.

and became addicted to brandy. Yet it is a remarkable fact that in all of Keats's letters, many of which are to his brothers and sisters, there is but a single reference to their mother, and this but a trifling one. (There is no mention at all of his father.) Keats was fifteen when his mother died (nine at the death of his father) so that he was certainly not without memory of her. We might suppose that in the normal course of things he would speak of her, that, in his tender letters to his sister Fanny, he would try to keep the mother's image alive in the little girl's mind. But we have not a word. There was much, it would seem, to be forgotten.

Yet it would also seem that there was much to be, in some fashion, remembered. Reynolds tells us that when John, at school, received the news of her death he was inconsolable. "When his mother died, which was suddenly—he gave way to such impassioned and prolonged grief—(hiding himself in a nook under the master's desk) as awakened the liveliest pity and sympathy in all who saw him." And George Keats, in a letter to Dilke, makes what is, I believe, the only significant reference by one of the Keats children to their mother: he says she "resembled John very much in the face, was extremely fond of him and humored him in every whim, of which he had not a few." He adds: "She was a most excellent and affectionate parent and as I thought a woman of uncommon talents."

We may take George's estimate of his mother as the expression of filial decency; or as the truth; or as some part of the truth. Yet there would seem to be no reason to question, there is indeed reason to suppose, her affectionate and indulgent nature— what we may call a biological generosity. It is then not difficult to understand the genesis of Keats's preoccupation with a felicity of "dainties," kisses, and coziness.

But how are we to understand the heroic quality of Keats, the quality of moral energy? In part, it is clear, by reference to Keats's temperamental endowment. We read of the violent child of five who armed himself with a sword and brandished it on guard at the door and refused to let his mother leave the house; the story in this form is given by Haydon, who is not reliable, though usually apt, in the stories he tells; another version of the story is that Keats used the sword to keep anyone from entering his mother's room when she was ill. We read of the schoolboy who would fight anyone—he offered to fight one of the ushers who had boxed his brother Tom's ears—and of whom it was said that anyone might easily fancy he would become great, but rather in some military capacity than in literature. The traits that make up what Plato calls the "spirited" part of the soul were early and extreme in Keats. But Keats himself made, as we may, a clear genetic connection between felicity and manly energy. He who had stood guard at the door—whether to keep his mother safe from invaders or to keep her captive—wrote in *Endymion* of the happy pastoral people of Latmos as those fair creatures "whose young children's children bred / Thermopylae its heroes," and omitted all mention of any intervening period of Spartan training. When he laid down the program of his development as a poet, he stipulated that the first phase of his life in poetry be devoted to sensual felicity as a prelude to his confrontation of the noble pain of existence.

It is possible to say of Keats that the indulgence of his childhood goes far toward explaining the remarkable firmness of his character, what I have spoken of as his heroic quality. This is not the occasion to engage upon a discussion of the theory of child-rearing. Such discussions, as conducted by laymen, and even as conducted by experts, are all too likely to be unmodulated, contrasting an unqualified indulgence or "permissiveness" with an equally unqualified disciplinary attitude. Indulgence is of many kinds and may be given in many contexts. Strength of character is also of different kinds, and it is necessary to ask what kind of strength our method of rearing seeks to inculcate. Thus there can be no doubt that a vigorous and strictly disciplinary training can indeed produce strength of a kind, even of an admirable kind. But, granting the complexity of the subject, I would yet venture to deal with it to the extent of proposing the idea that the person who was happily indulged as a child can in maturity—to use Keats's words—"bid these joys farewell" and "leave them for a nobler life," doing so of his own volition, with the moral advantages which attend upon free choice. His need of the childish joys has been satisfied, his will has not been fixed upon them.

"How strange it seems," says John Taylor after having retailed Mr. Abbey's account of Keats's parents, "that such a creature of the Elements as he should have sprung from such gross Realities —But how he refined upon the sensualities of his parents." How he refined indeed, but his relation to the "gross Realities" is not strange at all, or not strange in the way that Taylor meant. For the great and remarkable thing about Keats is that he did not refine by negation but by natural growth, by the tendency of life *to* refine. And when he had reached the top of the Platonic ladder of the appetites and had come as close as he could to what he called "fellowship with essence," he had no wish to kick over the ladder by which he had climbed. He felt free at any moment to climb down to the bottom-most rung, to put himself in touch with his first appetites. He was, as Taylor says, "a creature of the Elements," but he never forgot, as Taylor apparently did, that the elements include not only air, fire, and water, but also earth.

This license to put himself in touch with his first appetites, this unquestioning faith in pleasure, has played an important part in the developing estimate of Keats. It accounts for the need felt by certain of his partisans to insist that he was really a very manly young person. As the biographical and critical studies accumulate, the insistence is ever more strongly made, but even at its strongest it carries the implication that Keats was very manly *after all,* that we can see the manliness if we look close: the boy with his face pressed to the sweet-shop window is the image that persists, if only to be corrected.

But the fact is that Keats's mature masculinity is not something that is to be discovered by special perceptiveness. It is the essence of his being. One hesitates to say what one means by mature masculinity when the cultural anthropologists have been at such pains to disturb our old notions of it, and when in modern culture so much confusion exists about its nature and its value. Yet we may venture to say that in the traditional culture of Europe it has existed as an ideal that implies a direct relationship to the world of external reality, which, by activity, it seeks to understand, or to master, or to come to honorable terms with; and it implies fortitude, and responsibility for both one's duties and one's fate, and intention, and an insistence upon one's personal value and honor.

It is impossible to read Keats's letters without seeing that this was indeed his personal ideal. And the way he held it, the grace of his holding it, suggests to me that it grew easily and gently out of his happy relation with his infant appetites. To insist upon the growth of this ideal as a natural thing, and upon its not having negated what it grew out of, is not to deny all conflict. After all, Keats did institute a kind of antagonism between the idea of luxury and the idea of energetic morality. But in a complex and difficult culture the development of personality, even at its easiest and most natural, proceeds always by conflict

—Freud speaks of the erroneous belief of laymen that all neuroses (i.e., psychic conflicts) "are entirely superfluous things which have no right whatever to exist." We may not unreasonably suppose of Keats that both the seductiveness and the disorderliness that attended his mother's biological generosity made conflict the more necessary and the more lively. But what is characteristic of Keats is that the conflict is never to the death, is never cruel. He seems never to have wished to injure or destroy any part of himself. The conflicting ideals seem to understand each other and to wish to come to terms with each other.

As good an instance as any of the firmness, the developed strength of Keats's character is his simple probity in money matters. Even to himself this simple virtue seemed of great significance. It was often necessary for him to draw upon his publishers, Taylor and Hessey, who treated him with a generosity which was no doubt made the easier for them by Keats's financial punctiliousness. To Taylor he writes of "the sense of squareness in me" and of his "desire to be correct in money matters." He generalizes upon this exactitude in a striking way: in August of 1819 he writes to Taylor explaining why, in taking an advance, he prefers to secure the money by a note endorsed by his friend Brown. "I must observe again," he says, "that it is not from want of reliance on your readiness to assist me that I offer a Bill; but as a relief to myself from too lax a Sensation of Life—which ought to be responsible, which requires chains for its own sake—duties to fulfill with the more earnestness the less strictly they are imposed."

I have referred to the remark made by an old schoolfellow that Keats was a boy whom anyone might easily have fancied would become great, but rather "in some military capacity than in literature." And there is indeed in Keats's character a sort of ideal military virtue whenever he confronts the difficulties of life. What he calls the "flint-worded" letter of August 16, 1819, to Fanny Brawne, is full of military references as he discusses their situation, his lack of money, his powers of work. "This Page as my eye skims over it I see is excessively unloverlike and ungallant—I cannot help it—I am no officer yawning in quarters." He is, that is to say, in action. He says he cannot, will not, be careless of his friends' money. "You see how I go on," he says, "like so many strokes of a Hammer. I cannot help it—I am impelled, driven to it. I am not happy enough for silken phrases, silver sentences. I can no more use soothing words to you than if I were at this moment engaged in a charge of Cavalry." He is hard at work—as he says, "in the fever." "I would feign, as my sails are set, sail on without interruption for a brace of Months longer." The sailing image is in his mind because he is about to tell Fanny of an incident of naval fortitude which had moved him to admiration: the ship in which he was sailing to Southampton had with its bowlines snapped the top of the mast of a Navy launch. "Had the mast been a little stouter they would have been upset. In so trifling an event I could not help admiring our Seamen—neither officer nor man in the whole Boat moved a Muscle—they scarcely notic'd it even with words—Forgive me this Flint-worded Letter, and believe that I cannot think of you without energy of some sort—though mal a propos."

This is Keats's characteristic tone when he confronts the necessity of action. We know with what dread he contemplates the Italian journey, but, as he writes to Shelley, he will undertake it "as a soldier marches up to a battery," and he uses the same image to Taylor. Poetry was his life, yet when he wishes to praise poetry he says, "I am convinced more and more day by day that fine writing is next to fine doing the top thing in the world. . . ." With him the deed comes before the word. The deed is, as it were, the guarantor of the word. Even the dull action of getting a living was charged for him with heroic meaning. Disappointed in the expectation of a financial competence and faced with the necessity of supporting himself, he came to understand that he could live only by his own exertions and self-denial. "I had got into the habit of looking towards you as a help in all difficulties," he writes to Brown. "This very habit would be the parent of idleness and difficulties. You will see it as a duty I owe myself to break the neck of it. I do nothing for my subsistence—make no exertion. At the end of another year you shall applaud me not for verses but for conduct." He was one, as he had said some years before, to "volunteer for uncomfortable hours." He had that in him "which would bear the buffets of the world."

The remarkable statement to Fanny Brawne, "I cannot think of you without some sort of energy," tells us much. Energy is of his essence. It is the basis of his conception of morality, although it may transcend morality. "Though a quarrel in the Streets is a thing to be hated, the energies displayed in it are fine; the commonest Man shows a grace in his quarrel— By a Superior being our reasonings may take the same tone—though erroneous they may be fine."

In his own life he recognizes two states of being which would seem equally opposed to energy. One is what he calls "agonie ennuiyeuse" or despair—"I must choose," he says, "between despair and Energy." The other is a happy passivity, what he calls indolence—"a sort of temper indolent and supremely careless" —or languor or laziness: "If I had teeth of pearl and the breath of lillies I should call it languor—but as I am [his own footnote

here: "Especially as I have a black eye"] I must call it laziness."
And he goes on: "In this state of effeminacy the fibres of the
brain are relaxed in common with the rest of the body, and to
such a happy degree that pleasure has no show of enticement
and pain no unbearable frown."

"Agonie ennuiyeuse" is, of course, spleen, or melancholy, or
acedia: it is the very opposite of energy. But there is no real
antagonism between Keats's "indolence" and his energy. Keats's
great statement of the principle of passivity is contained in the
marvelous letter to Reynolds of February 19, 1818. This letter,
unpremeditated as it is, has the effect of a work of contrived art
as it accumulates its similitudes and intensifies its meaning until
at last it becomes incandescent in the lovely blank-verse sonnet
of the thrush, with its reiterated "O fret not after knowledge—I
have none." It is the exposition of the principle of the *power* of
passivity, of what Keats calls "diligent Indolence." The passivity
in question is of course related to Wordsworth's "wise passiveness," but it is far more richly characterized. Significantly
enough, it is characterized in a sexual way: "Who shall say
between Man and Woman which is the most delighted?"—
that is, in the sexual act.[5] And he has in mind the power of
conception, incubation, gestation. It is not the least remarkable
thing about Keats that, for all his "tendency to class women in
my books with roses and sweetmeats,—they never see themselves
dominant," he had an awareness, rare in our culture, of the
female principle as a power, an energy. He does not shrink from
experiencing its manifestation in himself, believing it to be

---

[5] It is perhaps worth recalling that an answer to this question is given in the classical
dictionary which Keats used—Lemprière's. Tiresias, who had been transformed into
a woman and then, after some years, restored to his original sex, was asked to settle
a dispute between Juno and Jupiter and gave it as his opinion that women have ten
times the pleasure of men. This so angered Juno that she deprived Tiresias of his
eyesight; in compensation Jupiter bestowed upon him the gift of prophecy.

half of his power of creation. Yet bold as he is in this, he must still assert the virtue of the specifically "masculine" energy: even the thrush assures him that "he's awake who thinks himself asleep," that by being conscious of his surrender to the passive, unconscious life he has affirmed the active principle.

## [ 5 ]

The dialectic which Keats instituted between passivity and activity presents itself in another form, in the opposition between thought and sensation. The case against the notion that Keats was systematically anti-intellectual has been conclusively made by Professor Clarence Thorpe, but apparently for each new generation of readers the evidence of his hostility to intellect seems more dramatic and decisive than that of his almost extravagant respect for intellect. His having said, "Oh for a life of Sensation rather than Thoughts," his having with Lamb drunk confusion to Newton, his general concurrence in the antagonism to eighteenth-century rationalism which prevailed in his set, and perhaps especially what is usually understood to be the doctrine of "Lamia," are taken to lend sanction to the belief that Keats was uniformly hostile to the exercise of the conscious mind. But Keats is far less simple than this would make him out to be. The injunction of the thrush's song, "O fret not after knowledge," had great authority with him, yet he did fret after knowledge and thought it right to do so. When he speaks of applying himself energetically to poetry, he conceives of that application as being in part to reading and study. "I know nothing, I have read nothing and I mean to follow Solomon's direction of 'get Wisdom—get understanding'—I find cavalier days are gone by. I find that I can have no enjoyment in the World but a continual drinking of Knowledge— . . .

There is one way for me—the road lies through application, study and thought."

The idea that Keats was anti-intellectual used to be easier to maintain when it was believed that, as one nineteenth-century critic put it, "Keats had no mind." To us the power of his mind is even more astonishing than the opinion that he had none, and we can scarcely be surprised that he should delight in its exercise. He did not think that difficult or abstract reading could corrupt his poetic impulse, and he was glad that he had kept his medical books; he found "every department of Knowledge . . . excellent and calculated towards a great whole." He conceived the emotional effect of knowledge to be analogous to that of poetry, which for him was successful when it led the reader to calmness. "An extensive knowledge is needful to thinking people—it takes away the heat and fever; and helps by widening speculation to ease the Border of the mystery." He said that "high Sensations" without knowledge induced anxiety—"horror"—but knowledge prevented fear. His judgment of his "Isabella" is that it has "too much inexperience of life and simplicity of knowledge in it."

He could, as we have seen, rate poetry inferior to action; he could also rate it inferior to philosophy. In the passage already referred to, in which he talks about how the charm of energy may be thought to redeem error, he says, "This is the very thing in which consists poetry; and if so it is not so fine a thing as philosophy— For the same reason that an eagle is not so fine a thing as a truth." He then goes on to say that he now understands from experience the force of Milton's line, "how charming is divine Philosophy." To Keats ideas were what Milton said they were, "musical as Apollo's lute," and he conceived that in heaven, where the potentiality of all things is realized, the nightingale will sing "not as a senseless tranced thing" but will utter philosophic truth.

If Keats did not accept the traditional antagonism between sensation and poetry on the one hand and intellect and knowledge on the other, it was because he understood intellect and knowledge in a certain way. He did not, that is, suppose that mind was an entity different in kind from and hostile to the sensations and emotions. Rather, mind came into being when the sensations and emotions were checked by external resistance or by conflict with each other, when, to use the language of Freud, the pleasure principle is confronted by the reality principle. Now, in Keats the reality principle was very strong. Was it ever by anyone more starkly asserted than in the phrase he used to Fanny Brawne: "I would mention that there are impossibilities in this world"? And it was strong in proportion to the strength of the pleasure principle. Philosophy and knowledge, the matter of the intellect, were for him associated in their old traditional way with the burden of life: to be "philosophical" means to acknowledge with the mind the pain of the world, and it means to derive courage from taking thought. "Until we are sick, we understand not;—in fine, as Byron says, 'Knowledge is Sorrow'; and I go on to say 'Sorrow is Wisdom.'" [6]

But the sentence does not end here. It goes on: "—and further for ought we know for certainty 'Wisdom is folly'!" This is perhaps a mere flourish to dismiss the subject. But it is also something more. It is an instance of Keats's urge toward the dialectical view of any large question, of his refusal to be fixed in a final judgment. As such it points toward that faculty of the mind to which Keats gave the name of "Negative Capability."

No one reading the letters of Keats can come on the phrase

[6] Byron actually said, "Sorrow is knowledge." (*Manfred* I. i. 10.)

and its definition without feeling that among the many impressive utterances of the letters this one is especially momentous. It is, indeed, not too much to say that the power and quality of Keats's mind concentrate in this phrase, as does the energy of his heroism, for the conception of Negative Capability leads us to Keats's transactions with the problem of evil, and to know the high temper of his mind we must follow where it leads.

## [ 6 ]

On the twenty-first of December, 1817, Keats wrote to his brothers, telling them, among other things, of his having gone to the Christmas pantomime with his friends Brown and Dilke and that, while walking home with them, he had what he called "not a dispute but a disquisition" with Dilke. The disquisition touched on "various subjects" which are not specified, and Keats says that as it proceeded "several things dove-tailed in my mind and at once it struck me what quality went to make a man of Achievement, especially in literature. . . . I mean *Negative Capability,* that is, when a man is capable of being in uncertainties, mysteries, doubts, without any irritable reaching after fact and reason."

In an ideological age such as ours the faculty of Negative Capability is a rare one, and Keats's naming and defining it attracts a good deal of notice either for praise or blame. It is often misunderstood. Thus, it is sometimes taken to mean that poetry should have no traffic with ideas, and that the creative writer is exempt from the judgment of intellectual validity. This is not in the least Keats's intention. Keats thinks of Negative Capability as, precisely, an element of intellectual power. At a later time, taking up the subject again,[7] he says, "the only means of strengthening one's intellect is to make up one's mind about

[7] But he never uses the famous phrase again.

nothing—to let the mind be a thoroughfare for all thoughts. Not a select party. . . ."

But this statement, although it clears away any doubts of the specifically intellectual nature of Negative Capability, is in itself very questionable. On its face it is obviously not true—it is certainly not true that "to make up one's mind about nothing" is the only means of strengthening one's intellect. Exclusion is quite as much a part of the intellectual process as inclusion, and making up one's mind is not only the end of intellection but one of the means of intellection. Yet Keats's statement may well be true in reference to a certain kind of person and to a certain kind of problem—to a certain kind of person dealing with a certain kind of problem. It is essential to an understanding of what Keats meant that we have in mind the kind of person who was Keats's interlocutor in the "disquisition" during which the idea came to him, and also the kind of problem that was at the moment preoccupying Keats's thought.

Charles Wentworth Dilke was a man whom Keats knew to be not only very good but very intelligent. But Keats was of the settled opinion that Dilke was far too doctrinaire in his intellect. He calls him a "Godwin perfectibility man," and because it is not only the doctrine of human perfectibility that is important in his judgment of Dilke—although it is *very* important—but also the over-systematic process of thought by which the doctrine is arrived at and maintained, he calls Dilke a "Godwin methodist." And he says of his friend that he "will never come at a truth so long as he lives; because he is always trying at it." This is a habit of mind which Dilke shares with Coleridge—in the passage in which Keats formulates the idea of Negative Capability, he cites Coleridge as an example of "irritable reaching after fact and reason." Coleridge, he says, was incapable of "remaining content with half-knowledge."

We are aware of a simple paradox, for traditionally truth must be striven for—*ad astra per aspera*. And half-knowledge is a sciolist's knowledge and "a dangerous thing." But we must consider the particular kind of problem to which the exercise of Negative Capability is appropriate. It will not be a scientific problem (although more than one great discoverer in science has said that at times it is well to suspend the irritable reaching after fact and reason, to let the mind be a thoroughfare for all thoughts or no thoughts, that then the data often speak unbidden). It will be a human problem—Shakespeare is Keats's example of a mind content with half-knowledge, "capable of being in uncertainties, mysteries, doubts." And in point of fact it is a particular and very large human problem, nothing less than the problem of evil.

This becomes apparent if we follow the line of thought that has been begun earlier in the letter. Before writing about the Christmas pantomime and Negative Capability, Keats tells his brothers that he has been to see Benjamin West's picture, "Death on the Pale Horse." He says that "it is a wonderful picture, when West's age is considered" (West was nearly eighty), but that he does not really admire it. One objection to it that he makes is that "there is nothing to be intense upon; no woman one feels mad to kiss, no face smiling into reality." Another objection is the artist's way of handling what Keats calls "disagreeables." "The excellence of every art," he says, "is its intensity, capable of making all disagreeables evaporate, from their being in close relation with Beauty and Truth. Examine 'King Lear,' and you will find this exemplified throughout, but in this picture we have unpleasantness without any momentous depth of speculation excited in which to bury its repulsiveness." And this theme is picked up again when Keats brings to an end his definition of Negative Capability: when he has made the famous remark about half-knowledge and remaining in "uncertainties, mysteries, doubts," he says that the subject, if "pursued through volumes would perhaps take us not further than this, that with a great poet the sense of Beauty overcomes every other consideration, or rather obliterates all consideration."

With this sentence we are at the very center of Keats's theory of art. It is a theory of extreme complexity and I shall not attempt to deal with it here. But the element of the theory that chiefly makes for its complexity—and its power—must at least be mentioned. Keats's theory of art is, among other things, an effort to deal with the problem of evil.

A contemporary literate mind is likely to be made uncomfortable by certain of the things that Keats says about the representation of evil in art, by the open resistance he makes to "disagreeables." We find him, for example, in "Sleep and Poetry," being very harsh with certain of his contemporaries, Byron in particular, over the subjects of their poetry. The themes, he says, are ugly clubs, the poets Polyphemes. And he quite shocks the modern literate mind by requiring of poetry that it should not "feed upon the burrs and thorns of life" and by judging those poets to be most worthy of respect "who simply tell the most heart-easing things." This is an opinion that will seem to us to have been dredged up from the depths of Philistinism. We can scarcely understand how a true poet, let alone a great poet, could have uttered it.

Similarly, when Keats concludes his remarks about Negative Capability with the observation that "with a great poet the sense of Beauty overcomes every other consideration, or rather obliterates all consideration," meaning all considerations of what is disagreeable or painful, it may seem that he has evaded the issue, that, having raised the question of painful truth in art, he betrays it to beauty in a statement that really has no meaning.

It is in this way that many readers understand the concluding
aphorism, the "moral," of the "Ode to a Grecian Urn"—out of
politeness to poetry they may consent to be teased, but they cannot suppose that they are enlightened by the statement, "Beauty
is truth, truth beauty," for, as they say, beauty is not all of truth,
and not all truth is beautiful. Nor will they be the more disposed
to find meaning in the notorious aphorism by the poet's extravagant assertion that in it is to be found "all/Ye know on
earth, and all ye need to know."

But the statement, "Beauty is truth, truth beauty," was not
for Keats, and need not be for us, a "pseudo-statement," large,
resonant, engaging, but without actual significance. Beauty was
not for Keats, as it is for many, an inert thing, or a thing whose
value lay in having no relevance to ordinary life: it was not a
word by which he evaded, but a word by which he confronted,
issues. What he is saying in his letter is that a great poet (e.g.,
Shakespeare) looks at human life, sees the terrible truth of its
evil, but sees it so intensely that it becomes an element of the
beauty which is created by his act of perception—in the phrase
by which Keats describes his own experience as merely a reader
of *King Lear,* he "burns through" the evil. To say, as many do,
that "truth is beauty" is a false statement is to ignore our experience of the tragic art. Keats's statement is an accurate description
of the response to evil or ugliness which tragedy makes: the
matter of tragedy is ugly or painful truth seen as beauty. To see
life in this way, Keats believes, is to see life truly: that is, as it
must be seen if we are to endure to live it. Beauty is thus a middle
term which connects and reconciles two kinds of truth—through
the mediation of beauty, truth of fact becomes truth of affirmation, truth of life. For we must understand about Keats that he
sought strenuously to discover the reason why we should live,
and that he called those things good, or beautiful, or true, which

induced us to live or which conduced to our health. (He had not walked the hospital wards for nothing.)

This way of seeing life, the poet's way, characterized by "intensity," is obviously anything but a "negative" capability— it is the most *positive* capability imaginable. But Keats understood it to be protected and made possible by Negative Capability: the poet avoids making those doctrinal utterances about the nature of life, about life's goodness or badness or perfectibility, which, if he rests in them, will prevent his going on to his full poetic vision.

At this point Keats's opinion of Dilke becomes important again. Keats believed that the Negative Capability which made possible the poetic vision of life depended upon a certain personal quality which he thought Dilke lacked. Of that poor Dilke who will never come at a truth so long as he lives because he is always trying at it, Keats says that he is "a man who cannot feel that he has a personal identity unless he has made up his mind about everything." Negative Capability, the faculty of not having to make up one's mind about everything, depends upon the sense of one's personal identity and is the sign of personal identity. Only the self that is certain of its existence, of its identity, can do without the armor of systematic certainties.[8] To remain content with half-knowledge is to remain content with contradictory knowledges; it is to believe that "sorrow is wisdom" and also that "wisdom is folly." It is not all of truth that Keats is concerned with but rather that truth which is to be discovered between the contradiction of love and death, between the sense of personal identity and the certainty of pain and extinction.

[8] This is only apparently contradicted by certain notable remarks which Keats made about men of genius in poetry *lacking* personal identity. (See the letter to Bailey of 22 November 1817 and the letter to Woodhouse of 27 October 1818.) In these passages he is speaking of the poet as poet, not of the poet as man.

Along with other of the English romantic poets, Keats is often said to have lacked an adequate awareness of evil and to have failed to see it as a condition of life and a problem of thought. I have indicated my belief that the contrary of this is true, that the problem of evil lies at the very heart of Keats's thought. But for Keats the awareness of evil exists side by side with a very strong sense of personal identity and is for that reason the less immediately apparent. To some contemporary readers it will seem for the same reason the less intense. In the same way it may seem to a contemporary reader that, if we compare Shakespeare and Kafka, leaving aside the degree of genius each has, and considering both only as expositors of man's suffering and cosmic alienation, it is Kafka who makes the more intense and complete exposition. And indeed the judgment may be correct, exactly because for Kafka the sense of evil is not contradicted by the sense of personal identity. Shakespeare's world, quite as much as Kafka's, is that prison cell which Pascal says the world is, from which daily the inmates are led forth to die; Shakespeare no less than Kafka forces upon us the cruel irrationality of the conditions of human life, the tale told by an idiot, the puerile gods who torture us not for punishment but for sport; and no less than Kafka, Shakespeare is revolted by the fetor of the prison of this world, nothing is more characteristic of him than his imagery of disgust. But in Shakespeare's cell the company is so much better than in Kafka's, the captains and kings and lovers and clowns of Shakespeare are alive and complete before they die. In Kafka, long before the sentence is executed, even long before the malign legal process is ever instituted, something terrible has been done to the accused. We all know what that is—he has been stripped of all that is becoming to a man except his abstract humanity, which, like his skeleton, never is quite becoming to a man. He is without parents, home, wife, child, commitment, or appetite; he has no connection with power, beauty, love, wit, courage, loyalty, or fame, and the pride that may be taken in these. So that we may say that Kafka's knowledge of evil exists without the contradictory knowledge of the self in its health and validity, that Shakespeare's knowledge of evil exists with that contradiction in its fullest possible force.[9] It is therefore not hard to understand the virtually religious reverence in which Shakespeare began to be held in the nineteenth century, for when religion seemed no longer able to represent the actualities of life, it was likely to be Shakespeare who, to a thoughtful man, most fully confronted the truth of life's complex horror, while yet conveying the stubborn sense that life was partly blessed, not wholly cursed.

Now Keats's attachment to the principle of reality was, as I have said, a strong one. He perceived the fact of evil very clearly, and he put it at the very center of his mental life. He saw, as he said, "too far into the sea" and beheld there the "eternal fierce destruction" of the struggle for existence, and the shark and the hawk at prey taught him that the gentle and habitual robin was not less predatory, that life in its totality was cruel; he saw youth grow pale and specter-thin and die, saw life trod down by life, the hungry generations on the march. For all his partisanship with social amelioration, he had no hope whatever that life could be ordered in such a way that its condition might be anything but tragic. He was not a theological mind like Kafka —some other adjective of large import must be used to suggest the scope and dignity of the questions with which he was preoccupied—yet evil presented its problem to him in the theological or quasi-theological form in which alone it has any meaning.

[9] It would, of course, be less than accurate and fair not to remark of Kafka that he had a very intense knowledge of the self through its negation, that his great and terrible point is exactly the horror of the loss of the Shakespearean knowledge of the self.

What is traditionally and technically called the problem of evil
raises a question about the nature of God, who is said to be both
benevolent and omnipotent, for man's experience of pain would
seem to limit either God's benevolence or his power. And the evil
which makes the problem truly a problem is neither that which
is the natural outcome of man's wrong deeds, nor that which
may be understood, by any human conception of justice, as divine punishment. In the Book of Job the problem of evil cannot
be really stated until the ground has been cleared of the conventional apologetics which try to explain Job's suffering as punishment for his sins: the divine voice itself says that the suffering is
not a punishment. For Dostoevski the problem of evil must be
stated in terms of the suffering of children—of human creatures,
that is, of whom we cannot say that their pain is the consequence
of their guilt. And Keats, who thought of women as exempt
from the moral life of men, and therefore not to be held responsible or guilty, conceives the problem of evil with particular reference to them. "Why," he asks, "should women suffer?" And
that *women* should "have cancers" is to him a conclusive instance of the unexplainable cruelty of the cosmos.

But at the same time that Keats had his clear knowledge of
evil, he had his equally clear knowledge of the self. Most of us
are conventional in our notions of reality and we suppose that
what is grim and cruel is more real than what is pleasant. Like
most conventionalities of thought, this one is a form of power-
worship—evil and pain seem realer to us than the assertions of
the self because we know that evil and pain always win in the
end. But Keats did not share in our acquiescence. His attachment to reality was stronger and more complex than ours usually
is, for to him the self was just as real as the evil that destroys it.
The idea of reality and the idea of the self and its annihilation
go together for him. "After all there is certainly something real

in the World—. . . . Tom [his brother] has spit a leetle blood this afternoon, and that is rather a damper—but I know—the truth is there is something real in the World." He conceives of the energy of the self as at least one source of reality. "As Tradesmen say every thing is worth what it will fetch, so probably every mental pursuit takes its reality and worth from the ardour of the pursuer—being in itself a nothing." And again: "I am certain of nothing but of the holiness of the heart's affections and the truth of the Imagination— What the Imagination seizes as Beauty must be truth—whether it existed before or not—for I have the same Idea of all our Passions as of Love they are all, in their sublime, creative of essential Beauty. . . . The Imagination may be compared to Adam's dream [in *Paradise Lost*]—he awoke and found it truth."

He affirms, that is, the creativity of the self that opposes circumstance, the self that is imagination and desire, that, like Adam, assigns names and values to things, and that can realize what it envisions.

Keats never deceives himself into believing that the power of the imagination is sovereign, that it can make the power of circumstance of no account. His sense of the stubborn actuality of the material world is as stalwart as Wordsworth's. It is, indeed, of the very nature of his whole intellectual and moral activity that he should hold in balance the reality of self and the reality of circumstance. In another letter to Bailey he makes the two realities confront each other in a very telling way. He is speaking of the malignity of society toward generous enthusiasm and, as he goes on, his thought moves from the life of society to touch upon the cosmos, whose cruelty, as he thinks of it, impels him to reject the life in poetry and the reward of fame he so dearly wants. "Were it in my choice," he says, "I would reject a petrarchal coronation—on account of my dying day and because women have cancers." But then in the next sentence but one: "And yet I am not old enough or magnanimous enough to annihilate self. . . ." He has brought his two knowledges face to face, the knowledge of the world of circumstance, of death and cancer, and the knowledge of the world of self, of spirit and creation, and the delight in them. Each seems a whole knowledge considered alone; each is but a half-knowledge when taken with the other; both together constitute a truth.

It is in terms of the self confronting hostile or painful circumstance that Keats makes his magnificent effort at the solution of the problem of evil, his heroic attempt to show how it is that life may be called blessed when its circumstances are cursed. This occurs in the course of his dazzling letter to George and Georgiana Keats in Kentucky which he began on February 14, 1819, and sealed on May 3. It is a massive journal-letter into which Keats copies, among lesser examples of his work, the sonnet "Why did I laugh to-night?," the two sonnets on fame, "La Belle Dame Sans Merci," the sonnet on sleep and the sonnet on rhyme, and the "Ode to Psyche." It is crammed full of gossip, personal, literary, and theatrical, and equally full of Keats's most serious and characteristic thought. The letter, indeed, is the quintessence of Keats's life-style, of his way of dealing with experience. It is one of the most remarkable documents of the culture of the century.

The climax of the letter occurs in the last full entry, that of April 15, in which Keats makes his dead-set at the problem of evil. This entry is the first after that of March 19, which in itself constitutes a very notable episode in Keats's intellectual life. The earlier entry is Keats's attempt to deal with the problem in aesthetic terms, as the later is his attempt to deal with it in moral terms. In the March 19 entry he writes that he is in a

state of languorous relaxation in which "pleasure has no show
of enticement and pain no unbearable frown," a condition which
he calls "the only happiness." But at the moment of setting this
down he receives a note from Haslam telling of the imminently
expected death of his friend's father, and he is led to speak of
the ironic mutability of life. "While we are laughing the seed
of some trouble is put into the wide arable land of event—while
we are laughing it sprouts it grows and suddenly bears a poison
fruit which we must pluck." Then follows a meditation on our
inability really to respond to the troubles of our friends and on
the virtue of "disinterestedness." This leads to the thought that
disinterestedness, so great a virtue in society, is not to be found in
"wild nature," where its presence, indeed, would destroy the
natural economy of tooth and claw. But from the spectacle of
self-interested cruelty of wild nature he snatches the idea of the
brilliance of the energies that are in play in the struggle for
existence. "This is what makes the Amusement of Life—to a
speculative Mind. I go among the Fields and catch a glimpse
of a Stoat or a fieldmouse peeping out of the withered grass—
the creature hath a purpose and its eyes are bright with it. I go
among the buildings of a city and I see a Man hurrying along—
to what? the creature hath a purpose and his eyes are bright
with it." He thinks of the disinterestedness of Jesus and of how
little it has established itself as against the self-interest of men,
and again he snatches at the idea that perhaps life may be justified by its sheer energy: "May there not be superior beings
amused by any graceful, though instinctive attitude my mind
may fall into, as I am entertained with the alertness of a Stoat
or the anxiety of a Deer? Though a quarrel in the Streets is a
thing to be hated, the energies displayed in it are fine; the
commonest Man shows a grace in his quarrel— By a superior
being our reasonings may take the same tone—though erroneous

they may be fine— This is the very thing in which consists
poetry—"

It is very brilliant, very fine, but it does not satisfy him;
"amusement," "entertainment" are not enough. Even poetry is
not enough. Energy is the very thing "in which consists poetry"
—"and if so it is not so fine a thing as philosophy— For the same
reason that an eagle is not so fine a thing as a truth."

"Give me credit—" he cries across the broad Atlantic. "Do you
not think I strive—to know myself? Give me this credit—" We
cannot well refuse it.

The simple affirmation of the self in its vital energy means
much to him, but it does not mean enough, and in the time
intervening between the entry of March 19 and that of April
15 his mind has been moving toward the reconciliation of energy
and truth, of passion and principle. He has been reading, he says,
Robertson's *America* and Voltaire's *Siècle de Louis XIV* and his
mind is full of the miseries of man in either a simple or a highly
civilized state. He canvasses the possibilities of amelioration of
the human fate and concludes that our life even at its conceivable
best can be nothing but tragic, the very elements and laws of
nature being hostile to man. Then, having stated as extremely as
this the case of human misery, he breaks out with sudden contempt for those who call the world a vale of tears. "What a little
circumscribed straightened notion!" he says. "Call the world if
you please 'The vale of Soul-making!' . . . I say *'Soul making'*
—Soul as distinguished from an Intelligence— There may be
intelligences or sparks of the divinity in millions—but they are
not Souls till they acquire identities, till each one is personally
itself."

There follows a remarkable flight into a sort of transcendental
psychology in the effort to suggest how intelligences become
souls, and then: "Do you not see how necessary a World of

Pains and troubles is to school an Intelligence and make it a Soul? A Place where the heart must feel and suffer in a thousand different ways." And the heart is "the teat from which the Mind or intelligence sucks its identity."

He writes with an animus against Christian doctrine, but what he is giving, he says, is a sketch of *salvation*. And for the purpose of his argument he assumes immortality, he assumes a deity who makes beings in an infinite variety of identities, each identity being a "spark" of God's "essence"; he assumes that the soul may return to God enhanced by its acquisition of identity. This assumed, "I began by seeing how man was formed by circumstances—and what are circumstances?—but touchstones of his heart—? and what are touchstones? but proovings of his heart? and what are proovings of his heart but fortifiers or alterers of his nature? and what is his altered nature but his Soul?—and what was his Soul before it came into the world and had these provings and alterations and perfectionings?—An intelligence—without Identity—and how is this Identity to be made through the medium of the heart? And how is the heart to become this Medium but in a world of Circumstances?"

The faculty of Negative Capability has yielded doctrine—for the idea of soul-making, of souls creating themselves in their confrontation of circumstance, is available to Keats's conception only because he has remained with half-knowledge, with the double knowledge of the self and of the world's evil.

[ 7 ]

So far as the idea of soul-making is doctrine—so far, that is, as it is something more than a moving rationale of heroism—it will probably not withstand the kind of scrutiny that today we are likely to give it. We have lost the *mystique* of the self. We cannot conceive of the self as having the same nature and the same value that Keats ascribed to it; we cannot respond to the justification of life by the heroic definition of self; and, having lost our knowledge of one term of Keats's equation, we are certain to find the reasons why his conclusion is wrong.

But when we deal adversely with Keats's notion of soul-making, we must at the same time deal with two greater poets than Keats. So far as Keats's resolution of the problem of evil is doctrinal, it leads us back to Milton. Here is Milton's characteristic doctrine of the conjoint nature of good and evil— "Good and evil we know in the field of this world grow up together almost inseparably. . . . Perhaps this is that doom which Adam fell into of knowing good and evil, that is to say, of knowing good by evil." Here is the Miltonic satisfaction at the expulsion from Eden, for from that great event all events follow, the life of "circumstances" has been instituted, history has been initiated, the human drama has begun, and now man may define his soul in the open and strenuous world of freedom as he never could in Eden—it is this, we feel, and not the great arguments of his theodicy that for Milton justify God's ways to man. And no one since Milton has put better and more feelingly the Miltonic doctrine of maturing freedom and responsibility in the field of this world than the young man who harked back incessantly to his Eden, to the primal bliss of satisfying the appetites without effort and without tears, who conceived the heroic vision of life because he first understood felicity.

Keats's doctrine of soul-making leads us not only to Milton, whose very theology was shaped by his love of the tragic poets, Shakespeare among them, but also to Shakespeare himself. What Keats calls "the bitter sweet of this Shakespearean fruit" is nothing else than the hard process of "provings and alterations and perfectionings" by which an "intelligence" acquires "identity" and becomes a "soul." The characterization of the "Shakespearean fruit" appears in the sonnet "On Sitting Down to Read 'King Lear' Once Again," and *King Lear* is precisely the history of the definition of a soul by circumstance. The sonnet begins with a farewell to "golden-tongued Romance with serene lute" —Romance is precisely not "circumstances." And what Keats says he is leaving Romance for is "the fierce dispute,/Betwixt Hell torment and impassion'd clay" [10]—between, that is, the knowledge of evil and the knowledge of self. We can understand why Keats's admiration of Shakespeare was so much more than a literary admiration, why Shakespeare had for him something of the magnitude of a religious idea, figuring in his letters as a sort of patron saint or guardian angel, almost as a Good Shepherd. Shakespeare suggested the only salvation that Keats found it possible to conceive, the tragic salvation, the soul accepting the fate that defines it.

Whether his heroic resolution of the problem of evil means much or little to us, we cannot doubt that to Keats himself it was a felt reality. It was not a doctrine formulated to guide his life if it might—rather it is a statement, as accurate as such a statement can be, of the nature of his being. It is impossible not to be moved to extreme pity by Keats's last days, by the young man doomed to death at the very moment that his genius has come into the full power that it had promised, at the moment too when he was at last able to feel the long-awaited passion of love. Sometimes he is buoyed up by the euphoria which is characteristic of his disease, but more often he is bitter, jealous, and resentful; the cup is being taken from him, and he is in despair. And yet, however great our pity may be, we cannot miss, unless we willfully and perversely wish to miss, the hard core of self

[10] The line appears so in the version of the sonnet in the Letters. Keats later revised "Hell torment" to "damnation."

which remains in the man. "I know the color in that blood—it is arterial blood—I cannot be deceived in that color; that drop is my death warrant. I must die." These are the words that he is reported to have uttered on the occasion of his first hemorrhage, and they suggest the heroic quality of his last days. He permitted nothing to be falsified. There are impossibilities in this world, and he knew them. His tortured fancy sometimes overpowered him—he imagined that Fanny Brawne might be unchaste, that Brown was not faithful, that the Hunts spied on him: his self was nearly maddened by the certainty of its extinction. Yet the dominant note is of fortitude, of courage, and of heroic concern for those he loved. As he lay on his deathbed, he asked Severn, "Did you ever see anyone die?" Severn never had. "Well then I pity you, poor Severn. What trouble and danger you have got into for me. Now you must be firm for it will not last long. I shall soon be laid in the quiet grave. Thank God for the quiet grave. . . ." And at the end: "Severn, lift me up, for I am dying. I shall die easy. Don't be frightened! Thank God it has come."

The tone, we feel, is not ours. To identify it we go back in time, and say, perhaps, that it is of the Renaissance, of Shakespeare. We do not have what produces this tone, the implicit and explicit commitment to the self even in the moment of its extinction. Events, it would seem, have destroyed this commitment—and there are those who will rise to say that it was exactly the romantic commitment to the self that has produced the dire events of our day, that the responsibility for our present troubles, and for the denial of the self which our troubles entail, is to be laid to the great romantic creators. And even those who know better than this will yet find it all too easy to explain why Keats's heroic vision of the tragic life and the tragic salvation will not serve us now. They will tell us that we must, in our time, confront circumstances which are so terrible that the soul, far from being defined and developed by them, can only be destroyed by them. This may be so, and if it is so it makes the reason that Keats is not less but more relevant to our situation. As we see him in his letters he has for us a massive importance —he has, as we say, a historical importance. He stands as the last image of health at the very moment when the sickness of Europe began to be apparent—he with his intense naturalism that took so passionate an account of the mystery of man's nature, reckoning as boldly with pleasure as with pain, giving so generous a credence to growth, development, and possibility; he with his pride that so modestly, so warmly and delightedly, responded to the idea of community. The spiritual and moral health of which he seems the image we cannot now attain by wishing for it. But we cannot attain it without wishing for it, and clearly imagining it. "The imagination may be compared to Adam's dream—he awoke and found it truth."

# Little Dorrit

*Little Dorrit* is one of the three great novels of Dickens' great last period, but of the three it is perhaps the least established with modern readers. When it first appeared—in monthly parts from December 1855 to June 1857—its success was even more decisive than that of *Bleak House*, but the suffrage of later audiences has gone the other way, and of all Dickens' later works it is *Bleak House* that has come to be the best known. As for *Our Mutual Friend*, after having for some time met with adverse critical opinion among the enlightened—one recalls that the youthful Henry James attacked it for standing in the way of art and truth—it has of recent years been regarded with ever-growing admiration. But *Little Dorrit* seems to have retired to the background and shadow of our consciousness of Dickens.

This does not make an occasion for concern or indignation. With a body of work as large and as enduring as that of Dickens, taste and opinion will never be done. They will shift and veer as they have shifted and veered with the canon of Shakespeare, and each generation will have its special favorites and make its surprised discoveries. *Little Dorrit,* one of the most profound of Dickens' novels and one of the most significant works of the nineteenth century, will not fail to be thought of as speaking with a peculiar and passionate intimacy to our own time.

*Little Dorrit* is about society, which certainly does not distinguish it from the rest of Dickens' novels unless we go on to say, as we must, that it is *more* about society than any other of the novels, that it is about society in its very essence. This essential quality of the book has become apparent as many of the particular social conditions to which it refers have passed into history. Some of these conditions were already of the past when Dickens wrote, for although imprisonment for debt was indeed not wholly given up until 1869, yet imprisonment for small debts had been done away with in 1844, the prison of the Marshalsea had been abolished in 1842 and the Court of the Marshalsea in 1849. Bernard Shaw said of *Little Dorrit* that it converted him to socialism; it is not likely that any contemporary English reader would feel it appropriate to respond to its social message in the same way. The dead hand of outworn tradition no longer supports special privilege in England. For good or bad, in scarcely any country in the world can the whole art of government be said to be How Not To Do It. Mrs. General cannot impose the genteel discipline of Prunes and Prisms, and no prestige whatever attaches to "the truly refined mind" of her definition—"one that will seem to be ignorant of the existence of anything that is not perfectly proper, placid, and pleasant." At no point, perhaps, do the particular abuses and absurdities upon which Dickens directed his terrible cold anger represent the problems of social life as we now conceive them.

Yet this makes *Little Dorrit* not less but more relevant to our sense of things. As the particulars seem less immediate to our case, the general force of the novel becomes greater, and *Little Dorrit* is seen to be about a problem which does not yield easily to time. It is about society in relation to the individual human will. This is certainly a matter general enough—general to the point of tautology, were it not for the bitterness with which the tautology is articulated, were it not for the specificity and the subtlety and the boldness with which the human will is anatomized.

The subject of *Little Dorrit* is borne in upon us by the symbol, or emblem, of the book, which is the prison. The story opens in a prison in Marseilles. It goes on to the Marshalsea, which in effect it never leaves. The second of the two parts of the novel begins in what we are urged to think of as a sort of prison, the monastery of the Great St. Bernard. The Circumlocution Office is the prison of the creative mind of England. Mr. Merdle is shown habitually holding himself by the wrist, taking himself into custody, and in a score of ways the theme of incarceration is carried out, persons and classes being imprisoned by their notions of their predestined fate or their religious duty, or by their occupations, their life schemes, their ideas of themselves, their very habits of language.

Symbolic or emblematic devices are used by Dickens to one degree or another in several of the novels of his late period, but nowhere to such good effect as in *Little Dorrit*. The fog of *Bleak House*, the dust heap and the river of *Our Mutual Friend* are very striking, but they scarcely equal in force the prison image which dominates *Little Dorrit*. This is because the prison is an actuality before it is ever a symbol;[1] its connection with the will is real, it is the practical instrument for the negation of man's

[1] Since writing this, I have had to revise my idea of the actuality of the symbols of *Our Mutual Friend*. Professor Johnson's biography of Dickens has taught me much about the nature of dust heaps, including their monetary value, which was very large, quite large enough to represent a considerable fortune: I had never quite believed that Dickens was telling the literal truth about this. From Professor Dodd's *The Age of Paradox* I have learned to what an extent the Thames was visibly the sewer of London, of how pressing was the problem of the sewage in the city as Dickens knew it, of how present to the mind was the sensible and even the tangible evidence that the problem was not being solved. The moral *disgust* of the book is thus seen to be quite adequately comprehended by the symbols which are used to represent it.

will which the will of society has contrived. As such, the prison haunted the mind of the nineteenth century, which may be said to have had its birth at the fall of the Bastille. The genius of the age, conceiving itself as creative will, naturally thought of the prisons from which it must be freed, and the trumpet call of the "Leonore" overture sounds through the century, the signal for the opening of the gates, for a general deliverance, although it grows fainter as men come to think of the prison not as a political instrument merely but as the ineluctable condition of life in society. "Most men in a brazen prison live"—the line in which Matthew Arnold echoes Wordsworth's "shades of the prison-house begin to close/ Upon the growing boy," might have served as the epigraph of *Little Dorrit*. In the mind of Dickens himself the idea of the prison was obsessive, not merely because of his own boyhood experience of prison life through his father's three months in the Marshalsea (although this must be given great weight in our understanding of his intense preoccupation with the theme), but because of his own consciousness of the force and scope of his will.

If we speak of the place which the image of the prison occupied in the mind of the nineteenth century, we ought to recollect a certain German picture of the time, inconsiderable in itself but made significant by its use in a famous work of the early twentieth century. It represents a man lying in a medieval dungeon; he is asleep, his head pillowed on straw, and we know that he dreams of freedom because the bars on his window are shown being sawed by gnomes. This picture serves as the frontispiece of Freud's *Introductory Lectures on Psychoanalysis*—Freud uses it to make plain one of the more elementary ideas of his psychology, the idea of the fulfillment in dream or fantasy of impulses of the will that cannot be fulfilled in actuality. His choice of this particular picture is not fortuitous; other graphic representations of wish-fulfillment exist which might have served equally well his immediate didactic purpose, but Freud's general conception of the mind does indeed make the prison image peculiarly appropriate. And Freud is in point here because in a passage of *Little Dorrit* Dickens anticipates one of Freud's ideas, and not one of the simplest but nothing less bold and inclusive than the essential theory of the neurosis.

The brief passage to which I make reference occurs in the course of Arthur Clennam's pursuit of the obsessive notion that his family is in some way guilty, that its fortune, although now greatly diminished, has been built on injury done to someone. And he conjectures that the injured person is William Dorrit, who has been confined for debt in the Marshalsea for twenty years. Clennam is not wholly wrong in his supposition—there is indeed guilt in the family, incurred by Arthur's mother, and it consists in part of an injury done to a member of the Dorrit family. But he is not wholly right, for Mr. Dorrit has not been imprisoned through the wish or agency of Mrs. Clennam. The reasoning by which Arthur reaches his partly mistaken conclusion is of the greatest interest. It is based upon the fact that his mother, although mentally very vigorous, has lived as an invalid for many years. She has been imprisoned in a single room of her house, confined to her chair, which she leaves only for her bed. And her son conjectures that her imprisoning illness is the price she pays for the guilty gratification of keeping William Dorrit in *his* prison—that is, in order to have the right to injure another, she must unconsciously injure herself in an equivalent way: "A swift thought shot into [Arthur Clennam's] mind. In that long imprisonment here [i.e., Mr. Dorrit's] and in her long confinement to her room, did his mother find a balance to be struck? I admit that I was accessory to that man's captivity. I have suffered it in kind. He has decayed in his prison; I in mine. I have paid the penalty."

I have dwelt on this detail because it suggests, even more than the naked fact of the prison itself, the nature of the vision of society of *Little Dorrit*. One way of describing Freud's conception of the mind is to say that it is based upon the primacy of the will, and that the organization of the internal life is in the form, often fantastically parodic, of a criminal process in which the mind is at once the criminal, the victim, the police, the judge, and the executioner. And this is a fair description of Dickens' own view of the mind, as, having received the social impress, it becomes in turn the matrix of society.

In emphasizing the psychological aspects of the representation of society of *Little Dorrit* I do not wish to slight those more immediate institutional aspects of which earlier readers of the novel were chiefly aware. These are of as great importance now as they ever were in Dickens' career. Dickens is far from having lost his sense of the cruelty and stupidity of institutions and functionaries, his sense of the general rightness of the people as a whole and of the general wrongness of those who are put in authority over them. He certainly has not moved to that specious position in which all injustice is laid at the door of the original Old Adam in each of us, not to be done away with until we shall all, at the same moment, become the new Adam. The Circumlocution Office is a constraint upon the life of England which nothing can justify. Mr. Dorrit's sufferings and the injustice done to him are not denied or mitigated by his passionate commitment to some of the worst aspects of the society which deals with him so badly.

Yet the emphasis on the internal life and on personal responsibility is very strong in *Little Dorrit*. Thus, to take but one example, in the matter of the Circumlocution Office Dickens is at pains to remind us that the responsibility for its existence lies even with so good a man as Mr. Meagles. In the alliance against the torpor of the Office which he has made with Daniel Doyce, the engineer and inventor, Mr. Meagles has been undeviatingly faithful. Yet Clennam finds occasion to wonder whether there might not be "in the breast of this honest, affectionate, and cordial Mr. Meagles, any microscopic portion of the mustard-seed that had sprung up into the great tree of the Circumlocution Office." He is led to this speculation by his awareness that Mr. Meagles feels "a general superiority to Daniel Doyce, which seemed to be founded, not so much on anything in Doyce's personal character, as on the mere fact of [Doyce's] being an originator and a man out of the beaten track of other men."

Perhaps the single best index of the degree of complexity with which Dickens views society in *Little Dorrit* is afforded by the character of Blandois and his place in the novel. Blandois is wholly wicked, the embodiment of evil; he is, indeed, a devil. One of the effects of his presence in *Little Dorrit* is to complicate our response to the theme of the prison, to deprive us of the comfortable, philanthropic thought that prisons are nothing but instruments of injustice. Because Blandois exists, prisons are necessary. The generation of readers that preceded our own was inclined, I think, to withhold credence from Blandois—they did not believe in his aesthetic actuality because they did not believe in his moral actuality, the less so because they could not account for his existence in specific terms of social causation. But events have required us to believe that there really are people who seem entirely wicked, and almost unaccountably so; the social causes of their badness lie so far back that they can scarcely be reached, and in any case causation pales into irrelevance before the effects of their actions; our effort to "understand" them becomes a mere form of thought.

In this novel about the will and society, the devilish nature of Blandois is confirmed by his maniac insistence upon his gentility, his mad reiteration that it is the right and necessity of his existence to be served by others. He is the exemplification of the line in *Lear*: "The prince of darkness is a gentleman." The influence of Dickens upon Dostoevski is perhaps nowhere exhibited in a more detailed way than in the similarities between Blandois and the shabby-genteel devil of *The Brothers Karamazov*, and also between him and Smerdyakov of the same novel. It is of consequence to Dickens as to Dostoevski that the evil of the unmitigated social will should own no country, yet that the flavor of its cosmopolitanism should be "French"—that is, rationalistic and subversive of the very assumption of society. Blandois enfolds himself in the soiled tatters of the revolutionary pathos. So long as he can play the game in his chosen style, he is nature's gentleman dispossessed of his rightful place, he is the natural genius against whom the philistine world closes its dull ranks. And when the disguise, which deceives no one, is off, he makes use of the classic social rationalization: Society has made him what he is; he does in his own person only what society does in its corporate form and with its corporate self-justification. "Society sells itself and sells me: and I sell society." [2]

[2] This is in effect the doctrine of Balzac's philosophical-anarchist criminal, Vautrin. But in all other respects the difference between Blandois and Vautrin is extreme. Vautrin is a "noble" and justified character; for all his cynicism, he is on the side of virtue and innocence. He is not corrupted by the social injustices he has suffered and perceived, by the self-pity to which they might have given rise; his wholesomeness may be said to be the result of his preference for power as against the status which Blandois desires. The development of Blandois from Vautrin—I do not know whether Dickens's creation was actually influenced by Balzac's—is a literary fact which has considerable social import.

Around Blandois are grouped certain characters of the novel of whose manner of life he is the pure principle. In these people the social will, the will to status, is the ruling faculty. To be recognized, deferred to, and served—this is their master passion. Money is of course of great consequence in the exercise of this passion, yet in *Little Dorrit* the desire for money is subordinated to the desire for deference. The Midas figure of Mr. Merdle must not mislead us on this point—should, indeed, guide us aright, for Mr. Merdle, despite his destructive power, is an innocent and passive man among those who live by the social will. It is to be noted of all these people that they justify their insensate demand for status by some version of Blandois's pathos; they are confirmed in their lives by self-pity, they rely on the great modern strategy of being the insulted and injured. Mr. Dorrit is too soft a man for his gentility mania ever to be quite diabolical, but his younger daughter Fanny sells herself to the devil, damns herself entirely, in order to torture the woman who once questioned her social position. Henry Gowan, the cynical, incompetent gentleman-artist who associates himself with Blandois in order to *épater* society, is very nearly as diabolical as his companion. From his mother—who must dismiss once and for all any lingering doubt of Dickens' ability to portray what Chesterton calls the delicate or deadly in human character—he has learned to base his attack on society upon the unquestionable rightness of wronged gentility. Miss Wade lives a life of tortured self-commiseration which gives her license to turn her hatred and her hand against everyone, and she imposes her principle of judgment and conduct upon Tattycoram.

In short, it is part of the complexity of this novel which deals so bitterly with society that those of its characters who share its social bitterness are by that very fact condemned. And yet—so much further does the complexity extend—the subversive pathos of self-pity is by no means wholly dismissed, the devil has not wholly lied. No reader of *Little Dorrit* can possibly conclude that the rage of envy which Tattycoram feels is not justified in some degree, or that Miss Wade is wholly wrong in pointing out to her the insupportable ambiguity of her position as the daughter-servant of Mr. and Mrs. Meagles and the sister-servant of Pet Meagles. Nor is it possible to read Miss Wade's account of her life, "The History of a Self Tormentor," without an understanding that amounts to sympathy. We feel this the more—Dickens meant us to feel it the more—because the two young women have been orphaned from infancy, and are illegitimate. Their bitterness is seen to be the perversion of the desire for love. The self-torture of Miss Wade—who becomes the more interesting if we think of her as the exact inversion of Esther Summerson of *Bleak House*—is the classic maneuver of the child who is unloved, or believes herself to be unloved; she refuses to be lovable, she elects to be hateful. In all of us the sense of injustice precedes the sense of justice by many years. It haunts our infancy, and even the most dearly loved of children may conceive themselves to be oppressed. Such is the nature of the human will, so perplexed is it by the disparity between what it desires and what it is allowed to have. With Dickens as with Blake, the perfect image of injustice is the unhappy child, and, like the historian Burckhardt, he connects the fate of nations with the treatment of children. It is a commonplace of the biography and criticism of Dickens that this reflects his own sense of having been unjustly treated by his parents, specifically in ways which injured his own sense of social status, his own gentility; the general force of Dickens' social feelings derives from their being rooted in childhood experience, and something of the special force of *Little Dorrit* derives from Dickens' having discovered its matter in the depths of his own social will.

At this point we become aware of the remarkable number of false and inadequate parents in *Little Dorrit*. To what pains Dickens goes to represent delinquent parenthood, with what an elaboration of irony he sets it forth! "The Father of the Marshalsea"—this is the title borne by Mr. Dorrit, who, preoccupied by the gratification of being the First Gentleman of a prison, is unable to exercise the simplest paternal function; who corrupts two of his children by his dream of gentility; who will accept any sacrifice from his saintly daughter Amy, Little Dorrit, to whom he is the beloved child to be cherished and forgiven. "The Patriarch"—this is the name bestowed upon Mr. Casby, who stands as a parody of all Dickens' benevolent old gentlemen from Mr. Pickwick through the Cheerybles to John Jarndyce, an astounding unreality of a man who, living only to grip and grind, has convinced the world by the iconography of his dress and mien that he is the repository of all benevolence. The primitive appropriateness of the strange—the un-English!—punishment which Mr. Pancks metes out to this hollow paternity, the cutting off of his long hair and the broad brim of his hat, will be understood by any reader with the least tincture of psychoanalytical knowledge. Then the Meagles, however solicitous of their own daughter, are, as we have seen, but indifferent parents to Tattycoram. Mrs. Gowan's rearing of her son is the root of his corruption. It is Fanny Dorrit's complaint of her enemy, Mrs. Merdle, that she refuses to surrender the appearance of youth, as a mother should. And at the very center of the novel is Mrs. Clennam, a false mother in more ways than one; she does not deny love but she perverts and prevents it by denying all that love feeds on— liberty, demonstrative tenderness, joy, and, what for Dickens is the guardian of love in society, art. It is her harsh rearing of her son that has given him cause to say in his fortieth year, "I have no will."

Some grace—it is, of course, the secret of his birth, of his being really a child of love and art—has kept Arthur Clennam from responding to the will of his mother with a bitter, clenched will of his own. The alternative he has chosen has not, contrary to his declaration, left him no will at all. He has by no means been robbed of his ethical will, he can exert energy to help others, and for the sake of Mr. Dorrit or Daniel Doyce's invention he can haunt the Circumlocution Office with his mild, stubborn "I want to know. . . ." But the very accent of that phrase seems to forecast the terrible "I prefer not to" of Bartleby the Scrivener in Melville's great story of the will in its ultimate fatigue.

It is impossible, I think, not to find in Arthur Clennam the evidence of Dickens' deep personal involvement in *Little Dorrit*. If we ask what Charles Dickens has to do with poor Clennam, what The Inimitable has to do with this sad depleted failure, the answer must be: nothing, save what is implied by Clennam's consciousness that he has passed the summit of life and that the path from now on leads downward, by his belief that the pleasures of love are not for him, by his "I want to know . . . ," by his wish to negate the will in death. Arthur Clennam is that mode of Dickens' existence at the time of *Little Dorrit* which makes it possible for him to write to his friend Macready, "However strange it is never to be at rest, and never satisfied, and ever trying after something that is never reached, and to be always laden with plot and plan and care and worry, how clear it is that it must be, and that one is driven by an irresistible might until the journey is worked out." And somewhat earlier and with a yet more poignant relevance: "Why is it, that as with poor David, a sense always comes crushing upon me now, when I fall into low spirits, as of one happiness I have missed in life, and one friend and companion I have never made?"

If we become aware of an autobiographical element in *Little Dorrit,* we must of course take notice of the fact that the novel was conceived after the famous incident of Maria Beadnell, who, poor woman, was the original of Arthur Clennam's Flora Finching. She was the first love of Dickens' proud, unfledged youth; she had married what Dickens has taught us to call Another, and now, after twenty years, she had chosen to come back into his life. Familiarity with the story cannot diminish our amazement at it—Dickens was a subtle and worldly man, but his sophistication was not proof against his passionate senti-mentality, and he fully expected the past to come back to him, borne in the little hands of the adorable Maria. The actuality had a quite extreme effect upon him, and Flora, fat and foolish, is his monument to the discovered discontinuity between youth and middle age; she is the nonsensical spirit of the anticlimax of the years. And if she is in some degree forgiven, being repre-sented as the kindest of foolish women, yet it is not without meaning that she is everywhere attended by Mr. F's Aunt, one of Dickens' most astonishing ideas, the embodiment of senile rage and spite, flinging to the world the crusts of her buttered toast. "He has proud stomach, this chap," she cries when poor Arthur hesitates over her dreadful gift. "Give him a meal of chaff!" It is the voice of one of the Parcae.

It did not, of course, need the sad comedy of Maria Beadnell for Dickens to conceive that something in his life had come to an end. It did not even need his growing certainty that, after so many years and so many children, his relations with his wife were insupportable—this realization was as much a consequence as it was a cause of the sense of termination. He was forty-three years old and at the pinnacle of a success unique in the history of letters. The wildest ambitions of his youth could not have comprehended the actuality of his fame. But the last infirmity of noble mind may lead to the first infirmity of noble will. Dickens, to be sure, never lost his love of fame, or of whatever of life's goods his miraculous powers might bring him, but there came a moment when the old primitive motive could no longer serve, when the joy of impressing his powers on the world no longer seemed delightful in itself, and when the first, simple, honest, vulgar energy of desire no longer seemed appropriate to his idea of himself.

We may say of Dickens that at the time of *Little Dorrit* he was at a crisis of the will which is expressed in the characters and forces of the novel, in the extremity of its bitterness against the social will, in its vision of peace and selflessness. This moral crisis is most immediately represented by the condition of Arthur Clennam's will, by his sense of guilt, by his belief that he is unloved and unlovable, by his retirement to the Marshalsea as by an act of choice, by his sickness unto death. We have here the analogy to the familiar elements of a religious crisis. This is not the place to raise the question of Dickens' relation to the Christian religion, which was a complicated one. But we cannot speak of *Little Dorrit* without taking notice of its reference to Christian feeling, if only because this is of considerable importance in its effect upon the aesthetic of the novel.

It has been observed of *Little Dorrit* that certain of Dickens' characteristic delights are not present in their usual force. Something of his gusto is diminished in at least one of its aspects. We do not have the amazing thickness of fact and incident that marks, say, *Bleak House* or *Our Mutual Friend*—not that we do not have sufficient thickness, but we do not have what Dickens usually gives us. We do not have the great population of characters from whom shines the freshness of their autonomous life. Mr. Pancks and Mrs. Plornish and Flora Finching and Flintwich are interesting and amusing, but they seem to be the fruit of conscious intention rather than of free creation. This is sometimes explained by saying that Dickens was fatigued. Perhaps so, but if we are aware that Dickens is here expending less of one kind of creative energy, we must at the same time be aware that he is expending more than ever before of another kind. The imagination of *Little Dorrit* is marked not so much by its powers of particularization as by its powers of generalization and abstraction. It is an imagination under the dominion of a great articulated idea, a moral idea which tends to find its full development in a religious experience. It is an imagination akin to that which created *Piers Plowman* and *Pilgrim's Progress*. And, indeed, it is akin to the imagination of *The Divine Comedy*. Never before has Dickens made so full, so Dantean, a claim for the virtue of the artist, and there is a Dantean pride and a Dantean reason in what he says of Daniel Doyce, who, although an engineer, stands for the creative mind in general and for its appropriate virtue: "His dismissal of himself [was] remarkable. He never said, I discovered this adaptation or invented that combination; but showed the whole thing as if the Divine artificer had made it, and he had happened to find it. So modest was he about it, such a pleasant touch of respect was mingled with his quiet admiration of it, and so calmly convinced was he that it was established on irrefragable laws." Like much else that might be pointed to, this confirms us in the sense that the whole energy of the imagination of *Little Dorrit* is directed to the transcending of the personal will, to the search for the Will in which shall be our peace.

We must accept—and we easily do accept, if we do not permit critical cliché to interfere—the aesthetic of such an imagination, which will inevitably tend toward a certain formality of pattern and toward the generalization and the abstraction we have remarked. In a novel in which a house falls physically to ruins from the moral collapse of its inhabitants, in which the heavens open over London to show a crown of thorns, in which the devil has something like an actual existence, we quite easily accept characters named nothing else than Bar, Bishop, Physician. And we do not reject, despite our inevitable first impulse to do so, the character of Little Dorrit herself. Her untinctured goodness does not appall us or make us misdoubt her, as we expect it to do. This novel at its best is only incidentally realistic; its finest power of imagination appears in the great general images whose abstractness is their actuality, like Mr. Merdle's dinner parties, or the Circumlocution Office itself, and in such a context we understand Little Dorrit to be the Beatrice of the *Comedy,* the Paraclete in female form. Even the physical littleness of this grown woman, an attribute which is insisted on and which seems likely to repel us, does not do so, for we perceive it to be the sign that she is not only the Child of the Marshalsea, as she is called, but also the Child of the Parable, the negation of the social will.

# Anna Karenina

W H E N *Anna Karenina* first appeared, it was read with a special delight which had as its chief element an almost childlike wonder at recognizing in art what was familiar in life. This, people said, is the way things are, the way they really are, the way we have always known them to be, and no writer has ever represented them so before. The general feeling about the book was expressed by Matthew Arnold when he said in his essay on Tolstoi that *Anna Karenina* was not to be taken as a work of art but as a piece of life. In any strict sense, of course, Arnold's statement is quite illegitimate—art is art and life is life; we read novels and live life; and if we try to express the nature of our response to certain novels by saying that we "live" them, that is only a manner of speaking. But it is a manner of speaking which is necessary to suggest the character of Tolstoi's art.

The early response to *Anna Karenina* had in it, I have suggested, a certain naïvety. It was as if people up to then had had experience only of an art which was formal and conventional and were now for the first time confronting an example of naturalistic representation, as if they had never before had the opportunity to perceive what verisimilitude was. Yet of course this was not at all the case. Tolstoi originated no new genre. When

*Anna Karenina* appeared—serially from 1875 to 1877 and as a volume in 1878—the novel as an art form had reached a very high point in its development and had made great conquests of that part of life with which the novel is pre-eminently concerned, the part of life which we call the *actual*. To mention only the novelists of France, where the theory of the actual had been more consciously formulated than anywhere else, Balzac had completed his great canon of French social history nearly three decades before, Flaubert had published both *Madame Bovary* and *L'Éducation sentimentale,* and Zola was in the full tide of his production. Yet with all these masters of actuality already on the scene—not to speak of his own *War and Peace,* which, although in the nineteenth century it did not have its modern reputation, was nevertheless much admired—Tolstoi still made with *Anna Karenina* the effect I have described.

And he continues to make it. In our time Proust and Joyce have greatly extended the dominion of the novel of actuality; our culture as a whole is obsessively committed to fact; we have removed virtually every taboo that once stood in the way of our grasp of the way things are and have evolved bold and elaborate sciences of human behavior which would have delighted Balzac and Zola. Yet still, when we read *Anna Karenina,* we exclaim in the old naïve wonder and surprise, Why *this* is the way it is, this is life itself! And a contemporary critic, Philip Rahv, in effect says for us today what Arnold said for the nineteenth-century readers of the book. In Tolstoi, Mr. Rahv says, "the cleavage between art and life is of a minimal nature. In a Tolstoian novel it is never the division but always the unity of art and life which makes the illumination. . . . One might say that in a sense there are no plots in Tolstoi but simply the unquestioned and unalterable process of life itself; such is the astonishing immediacy with which he possesses his characters that he can dispense with manipulative techniques, as he dispenses with the belletristic devices of exaggeration, distortion, and dissimulation."

This quality of lifelikeness, which, among all novelists, he possesses to the highest degree, does not make Tolstoi the greatest of novelists. Great as he is, there are effects which are to be gained by conscious manipulation and distortion, by plot and design, by sheer romancing, which he with his characteristic method cannot manage; there are kinds of illumination and delight which Tolstoi cannot give us but which Dickens, Dostoevski, and James can. But if Tolstoi is not the greatest of novelists—and that particular superlative, in any case, stands stupidly in the way of our free response to literature—he can be called the most *central* of novelists. It is he who gives to the novel its norm and standard, the norm and standard not of art but of reality. It is against his work that we measure the degree of distortion, exaggeration, and understatement which other novelists use—and of course quite legitimately use—to gain their effects.

Only one other writer has ever seemed to his readers to have this normative quality—what we today are likely to feel about Tolstoi was felt during the eighteenth century in a more positive and formulated way about Homer. It was what Pope felt when he said that Nature and Homer were the same.

One of the ways of accounting for the normative quality of Homer is to speak of his objectivity. Homer gives us, we are told, the object itself without interposing his personality between it and us. He gives us the person or thing or event without judging it, as Nature itself gives it to us. And to the extent that this is true of Homer, it is true of Tolstoi. But again we are dealing with a manner of speaking. Homer and Nature are of course not the same, and Tolstoi and Nature are not the same. Indeed, what is called the objectivity of Homer or of Tolstoi is not objectivity at all. Quite to the contrary, it is the most lavish and prodigal subjectivity possible, for every object in the *Iliad* or in *Anna Karenina* exists in the medium of what we must call the author's love. But this love is so pervasive, it is so constant, and it is so equitable, that it creates the illusion of objectivity, for everything in the narrative, without exception, exists in it as everything in Nature, without exception, exists in time, space, and atmosphere.

To perceive the character of Tolstoi's objectivity, one has only to compare it with Flaubert's. As the word is used in literary criticism, Flaubert must be accounted just as objective as Tolstoi. Yet it is clear that Flaubert's objectivity is charged with irritability and Tolstoi's with affection. For Tolstoi everyone and everything has a saving grace. Like Homer, he scarcely permits us to choose between antagonists—just as we dare not give all our sympathy either to Hector or to Achilles, nor, in their great scene, either to Achilles or to Priam, so we cannot say, as between Anna and Alexei Karenin, or between Anna and Vronsky, who is right and who is wrong.

More than anything else, and certainly anterior to any specifically literary skill that we may isolate, it is this moral quality, this quality of affection, that accounts for the unique illusion of reality that Tolstoi creates. It is when the novelist really loves his characters that he can show them in their completeness and contradiction, in their failures as well as in their great moments, in their triviality as well as in their charm. And what other novelist than Tolstoi, without ever abating his almost sexual love for his heroine, can make us believe of her, as we believe of Anna, that she has become a difficult, almost an impossible, woman? Or what novelist can tell us, as Tolstoi tells us of Vronsky, that his romantic hero is becoming increasingly bald without using the fact to belittle him? What we call Tolstoi's objectivity is simply the power of his love to suffer no abatement from the notice and account it takes of the fact that life usually falls below its ideal of itself.

It is a subtle triumph of Tolstoi's art that it induces us to lend ourselves with enthusiasm to its representation of the way things are. We so happily give our assent to what Tolstoi shows us and so willingly call it reality because we have something to gain from its being reality. For it is the hope of every decent, reasonably honest person to be judged under the aspect of Tolstoi's representation of human nature. Perhaps, indeed, what Tolstoi has done is to constitute as reality the judgment which every decent, reasonably honest person is likely to make of himself—as someone not wholly good and not wholly bad, not heroic yet not without heroism, not splendid yet not without moments of light, not to be comprehended by any formula yet having his principle of being, and managing somehow, and despite conventional notions, to maintain an unexpected dignity.

This is, of course, another way of saying that Tolstoi's reality is not objective at all, that it is the product of his will and desire (and of ours). And when we have said this, we must say more —we must grant that to achieve this particular reality Tolstoi omitted from it what some other realities include. Most notably he omitted the evil which is at the center of the vision of his great contemporary, Dostoevski. Tolstoi, to be sure, was anything but unaware of man's suffering. Levin, who, in *Anna Karenina,* is Tolstoi's representation of himself, is brought to a crisis of the soul by the thought that "for every man, and himself too, there was nothing but suffering, death, and forgetfulness," and he reaches a point where he believes that he "must either interpret life so that it would not present itself to him as the evil jest of some devil, or shoot himself." This is in form the very same idea that tortures Ivan Karamazov. But how different it is in tone, how different in intensity. Levin's sense of negation, though painful, is vague and perhaps merely melancholy; it has nothing of the specific horror and hideousness of Ivan's. And Levin can bring his crisis to resolution with relative ease, for he has conveniently at hand the materials of peace that Ivan does not possess and probably would not have accepted—piety, work, tradition, and the continuity of the family.

Nowadays the sense of evil comes easily to all of us. We all share what Henry James called the "imagination of disaster," and with reason enough, the world being what it is. And it is with reason enough that we respond most directly to those writers in whom the imagination of disaster is highly developed, even extremely developed. To many of us the world today has the look and feel of a Dostoevski novel, every moment of it crisis, every detail of it the projection of exacerbated sensibility and blind, wounded will. It is comprehensible that, when the spell of Tolstoi is not immediately upon us, we might feel that he gives us, after all, not reality itself but a sort of idyl of reality.

No doubt the imagination of disaster was not particularly strong in Tolstoi.[1] But perhaps it is just here that his peculiar value for us lies. For the imagination of disaster is a bold and courageous function of the mind but it is also exclusive and jealous—it does not easily permit other imaginations to work beside it; it more readily conceives evil than that to which the evil may befall; or, if it does conceive the thing that may be harmed, it is likely to do so in a merely abstract way. Our taste for the literature which arises from this imagination is a natural one, yet it has in it this danger, that we may come to assume that evil is equivalent to reality and may even come, in some distant and unconscious way, to honor it as such. Or it may happen that

---

[1] Although strong enough to give us the character of Levin's brother Nicolai, whose despair of life is as entire and as deeply rooted as that of any of Dostoevski's characters.

our preoccupation with evil will lead us to lose our knowledge, or at least the literary confirmation of our knowledge, of what goodness of life is. The literary production since Tolstoi has been enormously brilliant and enormously relevant, yet it is a striking fact that, although many writers have been able to tell us of the pain of life, virtually no writer has been able to tell us of pain in terms of life's possible joy, and although many have represented the attenuation or distortion of human relationships, scarcely any have been able to make actual what the normalities of relationships are. But in Tolstoi the family is an actuality; parenthood is a real and not a symbolic condition; the affections truly exist and may be spoken of without embarrassment and as matters of interest; love waxes and wanes, is tender or quarrelsome, but it is always something more than a metaphor; the biological continuity is a fact, not as in James Joyce's touchingly schematic affirmations, but simply and inescapably. It is, we may say, by very reason of the low pitch of his imagination of disaster that Tolstoi serves us, for he reminds us of what life in its normal actuality is.

I have said that it is chiefly Tolstoi's moral vision that accounts for the happiness with which we respond to *Anna Karenina*. That is why criticism, so far as it is specifically literary criticism, must lay down its arms before this novel. We live at a time when literary criticism has made for itself very bold claims which are by no means all extravagant. But the characteristic criticism of our time is the psychological analysis of language. This is a technique of great usefulness, but there are moments in literature which do not yield the secret of their power to any study of language, because the power does not depend on language but on the moral imagination. When we read how Hector in his farewell to Andromache picks up his infant son and the baby is frightened by the horsehair crest of his father's helmet and Hector takes it off and laughs and puts it on the ground, or how Priam goes to the tent of Achilles to beg back from the slayer the body of his son, and the old man and the young man, both bereaved and both under the shadow of death, talk about death and fate, nothing can explain the power of such moments over us—or nothing short of a recapitulation of the moral history of the race. And even when the charge of emotion is carried by our sense of the perfect appropriateness of the words that are used —Cordelia's "No cause. No cause"; or Ophelia's "I was the more deceived"; or Hamlet's "The rest is silence"—we are unable to deal analytically with the language, for it is not psychologically pregnant but only morally right; exactly in this way, we feel, should this person in this situation speak, and only our whole sense of life will explain our gratitude for the words being these and not some others.

In short, there are times when the literary critic can do nothing more than point, and *Anna Karenina* presents him with an occasion when his critical function is reduced to this primitive activity. Why is it a great novel? Only the finger of admiration can answer: because of this moment, or this, or this, mostly quiet moments, prosaic, circumstantial. Because of an observation of character: "Prince Kuzovlev sat with a white face on his thoroughbred mare from the Grabovsky stud, while an English groom led her by the bridle. Vronsky and his comrades knew Kuzovlev and his peculiarity of 'weak nerves' and terrible vanity. They knew he was afraid of everything, afraid of riding a spirited horse. But now, just because it was terrible, because people broke their necks, and there was a doctor standing at each obstacle, and an ambulance with a cross on it, and a sister of mercy, he had made up his mind to take part in the race." Or because of a fragment of social observation: "Vassenka Veslovsky had had no notion before that it was truly *chic* for a sportsman to be in tatters but to have his shooting outfit of the best quality. He saw it now as he looked at Stepan Arkadyevich, radiant in his rags, graceful, well-fed, and joyous, a typical Russian nobleman. And he made up his mind that the next time he went shooting he would certainly adopt the same get-up." Or because of Vronsky's unforgettable steeplechase and the almost tragic fall of the beautiful English mare; or Dolly's conversation with the peasant women about children and the business of being a woman; or Levin mowing with the peasants in the fields, the old peasant challenging him with "Once take hold of the rope, there's no letting it go!" and all the mowers watching for the master to break under the strain and on the whole glad that he does not; or the scene, taken from Tolstoi's own courtship of his wife, in which Levin and Kitty communicate by the initials of words written with chalk on a card table; or Alexei Karenin's determination to be a noble and Christian spirit and his inability to pursue his intention in the face of society's wish that he be ridiculous; or Anna's visit to her son on the morning of his birthday; or the passing of the moment in which Sergei, Levin's brother, might have proposed to Varenka, and the recognition by each of them that the moment had passed.

Part of the magic of the book is that it violates our notions of the ratio that should exist between the importance of an event and the amount of space that is given to it. Vronsky's sudden grasp of the fact that he is bound to Anna not by love but by the end of love, a perception which colors all our understanding of the relationship of the two lovers, is handled in a few lines; but pages are devoted to Levin's discovery that all his shirts have been packed and that he has no shirt to wear at his wedding. It was the amount of attention given to the shirts that led Matthew Arnold to exclaim that the book is not to be taken as art but as life itself, and perhaps as much as anything else this scene suggests the energy of animal intelligence that marks Tolstoi as a novelist. For here we have in sum his awareness that the spirit of man is always at the mercy of the actual and trivial, his passionate sense that the actual and trivial are of the greatest importance, his certainty that they are not of final importance. Does it sound like a modest sort of knowledge? Let us not deceive ourselves—to comprehend unconditioned spirit is not so very hard, but there is no knowledge rarer than the understanding of spirit as it exists in the inescapable conditions which the actual and the trivial make for it.

# William Dean Howells
## and the Roots of Modern Taste

[ 1 ]

Every now and then in the past few years we have heard that we might soon expect a revival of interest in the work of William Dean Howells. And certainly, if this rumor were substantiated, there would be a notable propriety in the event. In the last two decades Henry James has become established as a great magnetic figure in our higher culture. In the same period Mark Twain has become as it were newly established—not indeed, like James, as a source and object of intellectual energy, but at least as a permanent focus of our admiring interest, as the representative of a mode of the American mind and temperament which we are happy to acknowledge. To say that Henry James and Mark Twain are opposite poles of our national character would be excessive, yet it is clear that they do suggest tendencies which are very far apart, so that there is always refreshment and enlightenment in thinking of them together. And when we do think of them together, diverse as they are, indifferent to each other as they mostly were, deeply suspicious of each other as they were whenever they became aware of each other, we naturally have in mind the man who stood between them as the affectionate friend of both, the happy admirer of their disparate powers, who saw so early the fullness of their virtues which we now take for granted. It would make a pleasant symmetry if we could know that William Dean Howells has become the object of renewed admiration, that he is being regarded, like his two great friends, as a large, significant figure in our literature.

But the rumor of the revival is surely false. A certain number of people, but a very small number, do nowadays feel that they might find pleasure in Howells, their expectation being based, no doubt, on an analogy with the pleasure that is being found in Trollope. And the analogy is fair enough. Howells produced in the free Trollopian way, and with the same happy yielding of the rigorous artistic conscience in favor of the careless flow of life; and now and then, even in our exigent age, we are willing to find respite from the strict demands of conscious art, especially if we can do so without a great loss of other sanctions and integrities. Howells, it is thought, can give us the pleasures of our generic image of the Victorian novel. He was a man of principle without being a man of heroic moral intensity, and we expect of him that he will involve us in the enjoyment of moral activity through the medium of a lively awareness of manners, that he will delight us by touching on high matters in the natural course of gossip.

This is a very attractive expectation and Howells does not really disappoint it. He is not Trollope's equal, but at his best he is in his own right a very engaging novelist. Whether or not he deserves a stronger adjective than this may for the moment be left open to question, but engaging he undoubtedly is. And yet I think that he cannot now engage us, that we cannot expect a revival of interest in him—his stock is probably quite as high in the market as it will go. The excellent omnibus volume of Howells which Professor Commager recently brought out was piously reviewed but it was not bought. And when, in a course of lectures on American literature, I imagined that it might be useful to my students to have a notion of the cultural and social situation which Howells described, and therefore spent a considerable time talking about his books, I received the first anonymous letter I have ever had from a student—it warned me that the lapse of taste shown by my excessive interest in a dull writer was causing a scandal in the cafeterias.

As a historical figure, Howells must of course always make a strong claim upon our attention. His boyhood and youth, to which he so often returned in memory in his pleasant autobiographical books, were spent in circumstances of which everyone must be aware who wishes to understand the course of American culture. Howells' induction into the intellectual life gives us one of the points from which we can measure what has happened to the humanistic idea in the modern world. If we want to know what was the estate of literature a hundred years ago, if we want to be made aware of how the nineteenth century, for all its development of science and technology, was still essentially a humanistic period, we have only to take Howells' account of the intellectual life of the Ohio towns in which he lived—the lively concern with the more dramatic aspects of European politics, the circulation of the great English reviews, the fond knowledge of the English and American literature of the century, the adoration of Shakespeare, the general, if naïve, respect for learning. It was certainly not elaborate, this culture of little towns that were almost of the frontier, and we must not exaggerate the extent to which its most highly developed parts were shared, yet it *was* pervasive and its assumptions were general enough to support Howells in his literary commitment. In a log cabin he read to the bottom of that famous barrel of books, he struggled to learn four or five languages, he determined on a life of literature, and his community respected his enterprise and encouraged him in it. And it is worth observing that, as he himself says, he devoted himself to a literary career not so much out of disinterested love for literature as out of the sense that literature was an institutional activity by which he might make something of himself in the worldly way.

Howells' historical interest for us continues through all his developing career. His famous pilgrimage to New England, his round of visits to the great literary figures of Massachusetts, is a *locus classicus* of our literary history. It culminated, as everyone remembers, in that famous little dinner which Lowell gave for him at the Parker House; it was the first dinner that Howells had ever seen that was served in courses, in what was then called the Russian style, and it reached its significant climax when Holmes turned to Lowell and said, "Well, James, this is the apostolic succession, this is the laying on of hands." Much has been made of this story, and indeed much must be made of it, for although Holmes probably intended no more than an irony-lightened kindliness to a very young man, his remark was previsionary, and the visit of Howells does mark a succession and an era, the beginning of an American literature where before, as Howells said, there had been only a New England literature. Then Howells' uprooting himself from Boston to settle in New York in 1888 marks, as Alfred Kazin observes, the shifting of the concentrations of literary capital from the one city to the other. And when, as old age came on and Howells was no longer a commanding figure with the New York publishers, when he suffered with characteristic mild fortitude the pain of having his work refused by a new generation of editors, the culture of the American nineteenth century had at last come to its very end.

Howells' historical importance is further confirmed by the position he attained in the institutional life of American letters. Not long after Howells died, H. L. Mencken, who had been at pains to make Howells' name a byword of evasive gentility, wrote to regret his death, because, as he said, with irony enough but also with some seriousness, there was now no American writer who could serve as the representative of American letters, no figure who, by reason of age, length of service, bulk of work, and public respect, could stand as a literary patriarch. And since Mencken wrote, no such figure has arisen. Howells was indeed patriarchal as he grew older, large and most fatherly, and if he exercised his paternity only in the mild, puzzled American way, still he was the head of the family and he took his responsibility seriously. He asserted the dignity of the worker in literature at the same time that he defined the writer's place as being economically and socially with the manual worker rather than with the business man. He was receptive to the new and the strange; his defense of Emily Dickinson, for example, does him great credit. His personal and cultural timidity about sexual matters made him speak harshly of writers more daring in such things than himself, yet he fought effectively for the acceptance of contemporary European literature, and he was tireless in helping even those of the young men who did not share his reticences. Edmund Wilson once defined the literary character of Stephen Crane by differentiating him from "the comfortable family men of whom Howells was chief," yet Crane was in Howells' debt, as were Boyesen, Hamlin Garland, Norris, and Herrick.

He was not a man of great moral intensity, but he was stubborn. His comportment in the Haymarket affair marks, I think, the beginning in our life of the problem of what came to be called the writer's "integrity," and his novel *A Hazard of New Fortunes* is probably the first treatment of the theme which became almost obsessive in our fiction in the Thirties, the intellectual's risking his class position by opposing the prejudices of his class. Some years ago, it seemed appropriate for almost any academic writer on American literature to condescend to Howells' social views as being, in comparison with the tradition of revolutionary Marxism, all too "mild," and quite foolish in their mildness, another manifestation of his "genteel" quality. The fact is that Howells' sense of the anomalies and injustices of an expanding capitalism was very clear and strong. What is more, it was very *personal;* it became a part, and a bitter part, of his temperament. In his criticism of American life, he was not like Henry Adams or Henry James, who thought of America in reference to their own grand ambitions. Howells' ambitiousness reached its peak in youth and then compromised itself, or democratized itself, so that in much of his work he is only the journeyman, a craftsman quite without the artist's expectably aristocratic notions, and in his life, although he was a child of light and a son of the covenant, he also kept up his connections with the Philistines—he was, we remember, the original of James's Strether; and when such a man complains about America, we do not say that his case is special, we do not discount and resist what he says, we listen and are convinced. His literary criticism still has force and point because it is so doggedly partisan with a certain kind of literature and because it always had a social end in view.

It is of course in his novels that Howells is at his best as a social witness, and he can be very good indeed. The reader who wants to test for himself what were in actual fact Howells' powers of social insight, which have for long been slighted in most accounts of them, might best read *A Modern Instance,* and he would do well to read it alongside so perceptive a work of modern sociology as David Riesman's *The Lonely Crowd,* for the two books address themselves to the same situation, a change in the American character, a debilitation of the American psychic tone, the diminution of moral tension. Nothing could be more telling than Howells' description of the religious mood of the seventies and eighties, the movement from the last vestiges of faith to a genteel plausibility, the displacement of doctrine and moral strenuousness by a concern with "social adjustment" and the amelioration of boredom. And the chief figure of the novel, Bartley Hubbard, is worthy to stand with Dickens' Bradley Headstone, or James's Basil Ransom and Paul Muniment, or Flaubert's Sénécal, or Dostoevski's Smerdyakov and Shigalov, as one of a class of fictional characters who foretell a large social actuality of the future. Howells has caught in Hubbard the quintessence of the average sensual man as the most sanguine of us have come to fear our culture breeds him, a man somewhat gifted—and how right a touch that Hubbard should be a writer of sorts, how deep in our democratic culture is the need to claim some special undeveloped gift of intellect or art!—a man trading upon sincerity and half-truth; vain yet self-doubting; aggressive yet self-pitying; self-indulgent yet with starts of conscience; friendly and helpful yet not loyal; impelled to the tender relationships yet wishing above all to live to himself and by himself, essentially resenting all human ties. In the seventy years since *A Modern Instance* appeared, no American novelist has equaled Howells in the accuracy and cogency of his observation, nor in the seriousness with which he took the social and moral facts that forced themselves on his unhappy consciousness.

Yet if we praise Howells only as a man who is historically

interesting, or if we praise him only as an observer who testifies truthfully about the American social fact of his time, we may be dealing as generously and as piously with his memory as the nature of his achievement permits, but we cannot be happy over having added to the number of American writers who must be praised thus circumspectly if they are to be praised at all. We have all too many American writers who live for us only because they can be so neatly "placed," whose life in literature consists of their being influences or precursors, or of being symbols of intellectual tendencies, which is to say that their life is not really in literature at all but in the history of culture.

Perhaps this is the fate to which we must abandon Howells. The comparison that is made between him and Trollope, while it suggests something of his quality, also proposes his limitations, which are considerable. As an American, and for reasons that Henry James made clear, he did not have Trollope's social advantages, he did not have at his disposal that thickness of the English scene and of the English character which were of such inestimable value to the English novelists as a standing invitation to energy, gusto, and happy excess. Nor did he have Trollope's assumption of a society essentially settled despite the changes that might be appearing; his consciousness of the past could not be of sufficient weight to balance the pull of the future, and so his present could never be as solid as Trollope's. "Life here," as he said, "is still for the future—it is a land of Emersons—and I like a little present moment in mine." He never got as much present moment as the novelist presumably needs, and his novels are likely to seem to most readers to be of the past because nothing in America is quite so dead as an American future of a few decades back, unless it be an American personage of the same time.

And yet it is still possible that Howells deserves something

better than a place in the mere background of American literature. It is clear enough that he is not of a kind with Hawthorne,
Melville, James, and Whitman; nor of a kind with Emerson and
Thoreau; nor with Poe; nor with Mark Twain at his best. But
neither is he of a kind with H. B. Fuller and Robert Herrick,
whose names are usually mentioned with his as being in a line
of descent from him. If Howells is experienced not as he exists
in the textbooks, but as he really is on his own page, we have
to see that there is something indomitable about him; at least
while we are reading him he does not consent to being con-
signed to the half-life of the background of literature. For one
thing, his wit and humor save him. Much must be granted to
the man who created the wealthy, guilty, hypersensitive Clara
Kingsbury, called her "a large blonde mass of suffering," and
conceived that she might say to poor Marcia Hubbard, "Why,
my child, you're a Roman matron!" and come away in agony
that Marcia would think she meant her nose. And the man is
not easily done with who at eighty-three, in the year of his
death, wrote that strange "realistic" idyl, *The Vacation of the
Kelwyns,* with its paraphernalia of gypsies and dancing bears
and its infinitely touching impulse to speak out against the
negation and repression of emotion, its passionate wish to speak
out for the benign relaxation of the will, for goodness and gentleness, for "life," for the reservation of moral judgment, for the
charm of the mysterious, precarious little flame that lies at the
heart of the commonplace. No one since Schiller has treated
the genre of the idyl with the seriousness it deserves, yet even
without a standard of criticism the contemporary reader will,
I think, reach beyond the quaintness of the book to a sense of its
profundity, or at least of its near approach to profundity. It will
put him in mind of the early novels of E. M. Forster, and he

will even be drawn to think of *The Tempest,* with which it shares the theme of the need for general pardon and the irony of the brave new world: Howells, setting his story in the year of the centennial of the Declaration of Independence, is explicit in his belief that the brave newness of the world is all behind his young lovers.

When we praise Howells' social observation, we must see that it is of a precision and subtlety which carry it beyond sociology to literature. It is literature and not sociology to understand with Howells' innocent clarity the relationship of the American social classes, to know that a lady from Cambridge and the farmer's wife with whom she boards will have a natural antagonism which will be expressed in the great cultural issue of whether the breakfast steak should be fried or broiled. Again, when we have said all that there is to say about Howells' theory of character, have taken full account of its intentional lack of glory, we must see that in its reasoned neutrality, in its insistence on the virtual equality in any person of the good and the bad, or of the interesting and the dull, there is a kind of love, perhaps not so much of persons as of persons in society, of the social idea. At the heart of Herrick there is deadness and even a kind of malice. At the heart of Fuller there is a sort of moral inertness. But at the heart of Howells there is a loving wonder at the fact that persons of the most mediocre sort somehow manage to make a society.

I don't mean by this to define the whole quality and virtue of Howells but only to offer enough in his defense to make his case at least doubtful, because I want to ask the question, How much is our present friendly indifference to him of his making and how much is it of ours? It is a question which cannot be fully answered at this time but only in some later generation that is as remote from our assumptions as from Howells', yet it is worth attempting for what small self-knowledge the effort might bring.

## [ 2 ]

Henry James's essay on Howells is well known, and in that essay there are three statements which by implication define the ground of our present indifference to Howells. They have the advantage for our inquiry of appearing in the friendliest possible context, and they are intended not as judgments, certainly not as adverse judgments, but only as descriptions.

This is the first statement: "He is animated by a love of the common, the immediate, the familiar, and the vulgar elements of life, and holds that in proportion as we move into the rare and strange we become vague and arbitrary; that truth of representation, in a word, can be achieved only so long as it is in our power to test and measure it."

Here is the second statement: "He hates a 'story,' and (this private feat is not impossible) has probably made up his mind very definitely as to what the pestilent thing consists of. Mr. Howells hates an artificial fable, a denouement that is pressed into service; he likes things to occur as in life, where the manner of a great many of them is not to occur at all."

And here is the third: "If American life is on the whole, as I make no doubt whatever, more innocent than that of any other country, nowhere is the fact more patent than in Mr. Howells' novels, which exhibit so constant a study of the actual and so small a perception of evil."

It will be immediately clear from these three statements how far from our modern taste Howells is likely to be. I have said they are objective statements, that they are descriptions and not judgments, yet we can hear in them some ambiguity of tone—some ambiguity of tone must inevitably be there, for James is defining not only his friend's work but, by inversion, his own. And almost in the degree that we admire James and defend his artistic practice, we are committed to resist Howells. But I think we must have the grace to see that in resisting Howells, in rejecting him, we are resisting and rejecting something more than a literary talent or temperament or method. There is in Howells, as I have tried to suggest, an odd kind of muted, stubborn passion which we have to take account of, and respect, and recognize for what it is, the sign of a commitment, of an involvement in very great matters—we are required to see that in making our judgment of him we are involved in considerations of way of life, of quality of being.

His passion and its meaning become apparent whenever he speaks of the commonplace, which was the almost obsessive object of his literary faith. "The commonplace? Commonplace? The commonplace is just that light, impalpable, aerial essence which [the novelists] have never got into their confounded books yet. The novelist who could interpret the common feelings of commonplace people would have the answer to 'the riddle of the painful earth' on his tongue." We might go so far as to grant that the passion of this utterance has a kind of intellectual illumination in it which commands our respect, but we in our time cannot truly respond to it. We are lovers of what James calls the rare and strange, and in our literature we are not responsive to the common, the immediate, the familiar, and the vulgar elements in life.

Or at least we have a most complicated relation to these elements. In our poetic language we do want something that has affinity with the common, the immediate, the familiar, and the vulgar. And we want a certain aspect or degree of these elements in all our literature—we want them in their extremity, especially the common and vulgar. We find an interest in being threatened by them; we like them represented in their extremity to serve as a sort of outer limit of the possibility of our daily lives, as a kind of mundane hell. They figure for us in this way in *Ulysses,* in *The Waste Land,* in Kafka's novels and stories, even in Yeats, and they account, I believe, for the interest of comfortable middle-class readers in James Farrell's *Studs Lonigan.* In short, we consent to the commonplace as it verges upon and becomes the rare and strange. The commonplace of extreme poverty or ultimate boredom may even come to imply the demonic and be valued for that—let life be sufficiently depressing and sufficiently boring in its commonplaceness and we shall have been licensed to give up quiet desperation and to become desperately fierce. We are attracted by the idea of human life in, as it were, putrefaction, in stewing corruption—we sense the force gathering in the fermentation. But of course Howells' kind of commonness suggests nothing of this. The objection that many readers made to his early work was that it was drab and depressing, the point of comparison being fiction of plot and melodramatic incident, what Howells called the "romantic." But after a time the objection was to his tame gentility, the comparison being then with Zola. Howells admired Zola enormously and fought for his recognition, but he eventually thought that Zola failed in realism and surrendered to "romanticism." He meant that the matter of Zola's realism would lead his readers away from the facts of their middle-class lives. For Howells the center of reality was the family life of the middle class.

The feeling for the family with which Howells' theory of the commonplace was bound up was very strong in him, and Mr. Wilson is accurate when he makes it definitive of Howells' quality. His family piety seems to have amounted almost to a superstitiousness, for as such we must interpret his having said to Mark Twain, "I would rather see and talk with you than with any other man in the world," and then feeling it necessary to add, "outside my own family." His sorrows were family sorrows; after his marriage the direction of his life was given chiefly by the family necessities. All this, we may well feel, is excessive, and very likely it accounts for the insufficiency of personality, of self, in Howells that makes the chief trouble in our relation with him. He is too much the *pius Aeneas* without having Aeneas's sad saving grace of being the sire of an enormous destiny. Yet this must not lead us to lessen the credit we give to Howells for being the only nineteenth-century American writer of large reputation who deals directly and immediately with the family.

I do not know whether or not anyone has remarked the peculiar power the idea of the family has in literature—perhaps it has never been worth anyone's while to remark what is so simple and obvious, so easily to be observed from the time of the Greek epics and of the Greek drama down through the course of European literature. Even today, when our sense of family has become much attenuated, the familial theme shows its power in our most notable literature, in Joyce, in Proust, in Faulkner, in Kafka. But our present sense of the family is of the family in dissolution, and although of course the point of any family story has always been a threatened or an actual dissolution, this was once thought to be calamity where with us it is the natural course of things. We are sure that the nineteenth-century family was an elaborate hoax and against nature. It is true that almost every second-rate novel will represent one of its good characters expressing the hope of a quiet home and charming and satisfying children; it is true that the family is at the center of the essential mythology of our social and economic

life, the good and sufficient reason for accumulation and expend-
iture, and that the maintenance of the family in peace is the
study of our psychological science, yet in our literature the
family serves as but an ideality, a rather wistful symbol of peace,
order, and continuity; it does not exist in anything like actuality.

This may explain our feeling of indifference to the realism
of the commonplace. But our attitude toward the family must
be understood in a very large context, as but one aspect of our
attitude to the idea of *the conditioned,* of the material circumstances in which spirit exists. From one point of view, no people
has ever had so intense an idea of the relationship of spirit to
its material circumstances as we in America now have. Our very
preoccupation with *things,* as Mary McCarthy once observed, is
really a way of dealing with the life of spirit in the world of
matter—our possessions, although they have reference to status
and comfort, have a larger reference to the future of our souls,
to energy and the sense of cleanliness and fitness and health;
our materialism cannot be represented as the Roman *luxus* has
been represented—its style is not meant to imply ease and rest
and self-indulgence but rather an ideal of alertness and readiness of spirit. And this sense of the conditioned is carried out
in our elaborate theories of child-rearing, and the extravagant
store we set by education; and in our theories of morality and
its relation to social circumstance.

Yet it is to be seen that those conditions to which we do respond are the ones which we ourselves make, or over which we
have control, which is to say conditions as they are virtually
spirit, as they deny the idea of *the conditioned.* Somewhere in
our mental constitution is the demand for life as pure spirit.

The idea of unconditioned spirit is of course a very old one,
but we are probably the first people to think of it as a realizable
possibility and to make that possibility part of our secret assump-

tion. It is this that explains the phenomenon of our growing disenchantment with the whole idea of the political life, the feeling that although we are willing, nay eager, to live in society, for we all piously know that man fulfills himself in society, yet we do not willingly consent to live in a particular society of the present, marked as it is bound to be by a particular economic system, by disorderly struggles for influence, by mere approximations and downright failures. Our aesthetic sense—I mean our deep comprehensive aesthetic sense, really our metaphysics —which is satisfied by the performance of a Bendix washing machine, is revolted by such a politically conditioned society. The wide disrepute into which capitalistic society has fallen all over the world is justified by the failures and injustices of capitalism; but if we want to understand the assumptions about politics of the world today, we have to consider the readiness of people to condemn the failures and injustices of that society as compared with their reluctance to condemn the failures and injustices of Communist society. The comparison will give us the measure of the modern preference for the unconditioned— to the modern more-or-less thinking man, Communist society is likely to seem a close approximation to the unconditioned, to spirit making its own terms.

The dislike of the conditioned is in part what makes so many of us dissatisfied with our class situation, and guilty about it, and unwilling to believe that it has any reality, or that what reality it may have is a possible basis of moral or spiritual prestige, the moral or spiritual prestige which is the most valuable thing in the world to those of us who think a little. By extension, we are very little satisfied with the idea of family life—for us it is part of the inadequate bourgeois reality. Not that we don't live good-naturedly enough with our families, but when we do, we know that we are "family men," by definition cut off from the true realities of the spirit. This, I venture to suppose, is why the family is excluded from American literature of any pretensions. Although not all families are thus excluded—for example, the family of Faulkner's *As I Lay Dying* is very happily welcomed. And on every account it should be, but probably one reason for our eager acceptance of it is that we find in that family's extremity of suffering a respite from the commonplace of the conditioned as we know it in our families, we actually find in it an intimation of liberty—when conditions become extreme enough there is sometimes a sense of deep relief, as if the conditioned had now been left quite behind, as if spirit were freed when the confining comforts and the oppressive assurances of civil life are destroyed.

But Howells was committed totally and without question to civil life, and when he wrote an essay called "Problems of Existence in Fiction," although he did include among the existential matters that the novelist might treat such grim, ultimate things as a lingering hopeless illness, it is but one item among such others as the family budget, nagging wives, daughters who want to marry fools, and the difficulties of deciding whom to invite to dinner.

In extenuation of Howells we remember that this is all the matter of Jane Austen, the high reverberations of whose touch upon the commonplace we have habituated ourselves to hear. But Howells does not permit us to defend him with the comparison; he is profligate in his dealings with the ordinary, and in *A Hazard of New Fortunes* he does not think twice about devoting the first six chapters to an account of the hero's search for an apartment. I have heard that someone has written to explicate the place of these chapters in the total scheme of the novel, and in perfect ignorance of this essay I hazard the guess that its intention is to rescue Howells from the appearance of an excess of literalness and ordinariness, and that, in the carrying out of this intention, Basil March's fruitless ringing of janitors' bells is shown to be a modern instance of the age-old theme of The Quest, or an analogue of the Twelve Tribes in the Wilderness, or of the flight into Egypt, or a symbol of the homelessness of the intellectual. But it is really just a house-hunt. Of course any house-hunt will inevitably produce lost and unhappy feelings, even a sense of cosmic alienation—so much in our dull daily lives really does make a significant part of man's tragic career on earth, which is what Howells meant by his passionate sentence about the charm and power of the commonplace. But when we yield to our contemporary impulse to enlarge all experience, to involve it as soon as possible in history, myth, and the oneness of spirit—an impulse with which, I ought to say, I have considerable sympathy—we are in danger of making experience merely typical, formal, and *representative,* and thus of losing one term of the dialectic that goes on between spirit and the conditioned, which is, I suppose, what we mean when we speak of man's tragic fate. We lose, that is to say, the actuality of the conditioned, the literality of matter, the peculiar authenticity and authority of the merely denotative.[1] To lose this is to lose not a material fact but a spiritual one, for it is a fact of spirit that it must exist in a world which requires it to engage in so dispiriting an occupation as hunting for a house. The knowledge of the antagonism between spirit and the conditioned—it is Donne's, it is Pascal's, it is Tolstoi's—may in literature be a cause of great delight because it is so rare and difficult; beside it the knowledge of pure spirit is comparatively easy.

[1] Students have a trick of speaking of money in Dostoevski's novels as "symbolic," as if no one ever needed, or spent, or gambled, or squandered the stuff—and as if to think of it as an actuality were subliterary.

## [ 3 ]

To James's first statement about Howells, his second is clearly
a corollary—"He hates a 'story' . . . [he] hates an artificial
fable." We cannot nowadays be sure that all of our reading public loves a story in the way James did. Quite simple readers can
be counted on to love a story, but there is a large, consciously intelligent middle part of our reading public that is inclined to
suspect a story, in James's sense, as being a little dishonest.
However, where theory of a certain complexity prevails, the
implications of story, and even of "artificial fable," are nowadays easily understood. In these uplands of taste we comprehend
that artificial devices, such as manipulated plot, are a way not
of escaping from reality but of representing it, and we speak
with vivacity of "imaginary gardens with real toads in them."
Indeed, we have come to believe that the toad is the less real
when the garden is also real. Our metaphysical habits lead us
to feel the deficiency of what we call literal reality and to prefer
what we call essential reality. To be sure, when we speak of literal reality, we are aware that there is really no such thing—
that everything that is *per*ceived is in some sense *con*ceived, or
created; it is controlled by intention and indicates intention;
and so on. Nevertheless, bound as we are by society and convention, as well as by certain necessities of the mind, there still is
a thing that we persist in calling "literal reality," and we recognize in works of art a greater or less approximation to it. Having
admitted the existence of literal reality, we give it a low status
in our judgment of art. Naturalism, which is the form of art
that makes its effects by the accumulation of the details of literal reality, is now in poor repute among us. We dismiss it as
an analogue of an outmoded science and look to contemporary

science to give authority to our preference for the abstract and conceptual; or we look to music to justify our impatience with the representational; and we derive a kind of political satisfaction from our taste, remembering that reactionary governments hate what we admire.

Our metaphysical and aesthetic prejudices even conspire to make us believe that our children have chiefly an "essential" sense of reality. We characterize the whole bent of their minds by their flights of fancy and by the extremity of distortion in their school paintings, preferring to forget that if they are in some degree and on some occasions essential realists, they are also passionately pedantic literalists—as they must be when their whole souls are so directed toward accommodation and control. The vogue of the "educational" toy with its merely essential representation is an adult vogue; the two-year-old wants the miniature Chevrolet with as many precise details as possible; it is not the gay chintz ball designed for the infant eye and grasp that delights him but rather the apple or the orange—its function, its use, its being valued by the family, give him his pleasure; and as he grows older his pedantry of literalism will increase, and he will scorn the adult world for the metaphysical vagaries of its absurd conduct—until he himself is seduced by them.

Now we must admit that Howells' extravagance of literalism, his downright, declared hatred of a story, was on the whole not very intelligent. He said of Zola that "the imperfection of his realism began with the perfection of his form." That is, just where Zola appeals to us, just where he disregards his own syllabus of the experimental novel to introduce dramatic extravagance, he is disappointing to Howells. And Howells, in his character of programmatic literalist, spoke disrespectfully of Scott (one of the founders of realism), of Dickens, and of Balzac, saying that the truth was not in them; and he went so far as to express impatience with the romancing of George Eliot, despite the clear affinity his realism has with hers. It is difficult to know what he made of his adored Jane Austen. Clearly it never occurred to him, as he sought to learn from her, that some of her finest effects are due to her carefully contrived stories. We, of course, find it natural to say that the perfection of her realism begins with the perfection of her form.

It is perhaps an expression of our desire for unconditioned spirit that we have of late years been so preoccupied with artifice and form. We feel that the shape which the mind gives to what the mind observes is more ideally characteristic of the mind than is the act of observation. Possibly it is, and if the last decades of criticism have insisted rather too much that this is so,[2] it is possible that a view of our historical situation might lead us to justify the overemphasis, for in the historical perspective we perceive such a depressing plethora of matter and so little form. Form suggests a principle of control—I can quite understand that group of my students who have become excited over their discovery of the old animosity which Ezra Pound and William Carlos Williams bear to the iamb, and have come to feel that could they but break the iambic shackles, the whole of modern culture could find a true expression.

The value of form must never be denigrated. But by a perversity of our minds, just as the commitment to a particular matter of literature is likely to be conceived in terms of hostility to form, so the devotion to the power of form is likely to be conceived in terms of hostility to matter, to matter in its sheer literalness, in its stubborn denotativeness. The claims of form

---

[2] Who can imagine any of our critics saying with Ruskin that "No good work whatever can be perfect, and the demand for perfection is always a sign of a misunderstanding of the ends of art"; and ". . . No great man ever stops working till he has reached his point of failure . . ."?

to pre-eminence over matter always have a certain advantage because of the feeling to which I have just referred, that the mind's power of shaping is more characteristic of mind than its power of observation. Certainly the power of shaping is more intimately connected with what Plato called the "spirited" part of man, with the will, while observation may be thought of as springing from the merely "vegetative" part. The eye, it cannot choose but see, we cannot bid the ear be still; things impress themselves upon us against or with our will. But the plastic stress of spirit is of the will in the sense that it strives against resistance, against the stubbornness of what Shelley called the dull, dense world—it compels "all new successions to the forms they wear."

But Shelley's description of the act of creation suggests that the plastic will cannot possibly exercise itself without the recalcitrance of stupid literal matter. When we consider what is going on in painting at this moment, we perceive what may happen in an art when it frees itself entirely from the objective. No doubt the defense of the legitimacy of nonobjective art which is made by referring to the right of music to be unindentured to an objective reality is as convincing as it ever was. Yet do we not have the unhappy sense that sterility is overtaking the painters, that by totally freeing themselves from the objective reality which they believed extraneous to their art, they have provided the plastic will with no resisting object, or none except itself as expressed by other painters, and are therefore beginning to express themselves in mere competitive ingenuity? It is no accident of the *Zeitgeist* that the classic painting of our time is Cubism. The Cubists, bold as they were, accepted the conditioned, and kept in touch with a world of literality. And this is the opinion of one of the greatest of the Cubists, Juan Gris. "Those who believe in abstract painting," he wrote in a letter of 1919, "are like weavers who think they can produce material with only one set of threads and forget that there has to be another set to hold these together. Where there is no attempt at plasticity how can you control representational liberties? And where there is no concern for reality how can you limit and unite plastic liberties?"

What is true of the Cubists is also true of the great classic writers of our time—the sense of *things* is stronger in them than in their expositors. They grew in naturalism, in literalism, and they in their way insist on it as much as Flaubert, or the Goncourts, or Zola. The impulse of succeeding writers to build on Joyce is pretty sure to be frustrated, for it is all too likely to be an attempt to build on Joyce's notions of form, which have force only in relation to Joyce's superb sense of literal fact, his solid simple awareness that in the work of art some things are merely denotative and do not connote more than appears, that they are *data* and must be permitted to exist as data.

# [ 4 ]

The last of James's statements about Howells concerns his indifference to evil. For us today this constitutes a very severe indictment. We are all aware of evil; we began to be aware of it in certain quasi-religious senses a couple of decades or so ago; and as time passed we learned a great deal about the physical, political actuality of evil, saw it expressed in the political life in a kind of gratuitous devilishness which has always been in the world but which never before in Western Europe had been organized and, as it were, rationalized. A proper sense of evil is surely an attribute of a great writer, and nowadays we have been drawn to make it almost a touchstone of greatness, drawn to do so in part by our revived religious feelings or nostalgia for religious feelings, but of course also in part by our desire that literature should be in accord with reality as we now know it.

Our responsiveness to the idea of evil is legitimate enough, yet we ought to be aware that the management of the sense of evil is not an easy thing. Be careful, Nietzsche said, when you fight dragons, lest you become a dragon yourself. There is always the danger, when we have insisted upon the fact of evil with a certain intensity, that we will go on to cherish the virtue of our insistence, and then the very fact we insist upon. I would make a distinction between the relation to evil of the creator of the literary work and that of the reader, believing that the active confrontation of the fact of evil is likelier to be healthy than is the passive confrontation—there is something suspect in making evil the object of, as it were, aesthetic contemplation. But not even the creator is nowadays immune from all danger. Consider that the awareness of evil is held by us to confer a certain kind of spiritual status and prestige upon the person who exercises it, a status and prestige which are often quite out of proportion to his general spiritual gifts. Our time has a very quick sensitivity to what the sociologists call *charisma,* which, in the socio-political context, is the quality of power and leadership that seems to derive from a direct connection with great supernal forces, with godhead. This power we respond to when we find it in our literature in the form of alliances with the dark gods of sexuality, or the huge inscrutability of nature, or the church, or history; presumably we want it for ourselves. This is what accounts in our theory of literature for our preference for the hidden and ambiguous, for our demand for "tension" and "tragedy." And evil has for us its own *charisma.* Hannah Arendt, in *The Origins of Totalitarianism,* speaking of the modern disintegration, remarks that with us today "to yield to the mere process of disintegration has become an irresistible temptation, not only because it has assumed the spurious grandeur of 'historical necessity' but also because everything outside it has begun to appear lifeless, bloodless, meaningless, and unreal." Disintegration itself fascinates us because it is a power. Evil has always fascinated men, not only because it is opposed to good but also because it is, in its own right, a power.

*Lifeless, bloodless, meaningless,* and *unreal*—without stopping to estimate just how much life, blood, meaning, and reality Howells actually has, we must observe that the modern reader who judges him to have little is not exactly in a position to be objective, that he is likely to deal with Howells under the aspect of a universal judgment by which it is concluded that very little in our life has life, blood, meaning, and reality.

The sentence in which Howells invites American novelists to concern themselves with the "more smiling aspects" of life as being the "more American" is well known and has done much harm to his reputation. In fairness to Howells, we ought to be aware that the sentence may not be quite so dreadful as is generally supposed. For one thing, it is rather ambiguous—when Howells says "we invite," it is not clear whether "we" is the editorial pronoun referring to himself or is meant to stand for the American people: the phrase, that is, may be read as simply descriptive of a disposition of American culture. And even if we take the sentence in its worst construction, we ought to recall that it appears in an essay on Dostoevski in which Howells urges the reading of Dostoevski; that when he speaks of the more smiling aspects of life as being the more American it is in the course of a comparison of America with the Russia of Dostoevski; that he is careful to remark that America is not exempt from the sorrows of the natural course of life, only from those which are peculiar to the poverty and oppression of Dostoevski's land; and that he says he is not sure that America is in every way the gainer by being so thoroughly in material luck, so rich in the smiling aspects. But let us leave all extenuation aside and take the sentence only as it has established itself in the legendary way, as the clear sign of Howells' blindness to evil, his ignorance of the very essence of reality. Taken so, it perhaps cannot be thought a very wise statement, but our interpretation of it, the vehemence with which we are likely to press its meaning, tells us, I think, more about ourselves than about Howells. It raises the question of why we believe, as we do believe, that evil is of the very essence of reality.

The management of the sense of evil, I have said, is not easy. The sense of evil is properly managed only when it is not allowed to be preponderant over the sense of self. The reason Shakespeare holds his place in our imagination is that in him the sense of evil and the sense of self are in so delicate and continuous a reciprocation. And the ground of Keats's greatness, I have come to feel, is that precarious reciprocation of self and evil, similar to Shakespeare's. He maintained this reciprocation in a more conscious and explicit way than Shakespeare found necessary. He called to his aid in the affirmation of self against the knowledge of evil his intense imagination of pleasure—of pleasure of all kinds, the simplest and most primitive, such as eating and drinking, as well as the highest. He boldly put pleasure, even contentment, at the center of his theory of poetry, and at one point in the development of his theory he spoke of poetry as being most itself when it tells "heart-easing things." It is just for this reason that some readers denigrate him; they quite miss the intensity of his sense of reality, for where they make a duality of the principle of pleasure and the principle of reality, Keats made a unity—for him pleasure was a reality; it was, as Wordsworth had taught him, the grand principle of life, of mind, and of self. And it was this commitment to pleasure that made it possible for him to write the greatest exposition of the meaning of tragedy in our literature.

When we are so eager to say how wrong Howells was to invite the novelist to deal with the smiling aspects of life, we have to ask ourselves whether our quick antagonism to this mild recognition of pleasure does not imply an impatience with the self, a degree of yielding to what Hannah Arendt calls the irresistible temptation of disintegration, of identification by submission to the grandeur of historical necessity which is so much more powerful than the self. It is possible that our easily expressed contempt for the smiling aspects and our covert impulse to yield to the historical process are a way of acquiring charisma. It is that peculiar charisma which has always been inherent in death. It was neither a genteel novelist nor a romantic poet who most recently defended the necessity of the smiling aspects and the heart-easing things—Dr. Bruno Bettelheim was first known in this country for his study, made at first hand, of the psychology of the inmates of the German concentration camps. Dr. Bettelheim recently found occasion to remark that "a fight for the very survival of civilized mankind is actually a fight to restore man to a sensitivity toward the joys of life. Only in this way can man be liberated and the survival of civilized mankind be assured. Maybe a time has come in which our main efforts need no longer be directed toward modifying the pleasure principle. [Dr. Bettelheim is speaking of the practice of psychoanalysis.] Maybe it is time we became concerned with restoring pleasure gratification to its dominant role in the reality principle; maybe this society needs less a modification of the pleasure principle by reality, and more assertion of the pleasure principle against an overpowering pleasure-denying reality." It cannot be said of Howells' smiling aspects that they represent a very intense kind of pleasure; yet for most men they will at least serve, in Keats's phrase, to bind us to the earth, to prevent our being seduced by the godhead of disintegration.

## [ 5 ]

"Your really beautiful time will come," wrote Henry James to Howells on the occasion of his seventy-fifth birthday—what James characteristically meant was the time when the critical intelligence would begin to render Howells its tribute. The really beautiful time has come to James, but it has not yet come to Howells, and probably it will be a very long time coming. We are not easy with the quiet men, the civil personalities—the very word *civil,* except as applied to disobedience or disorders, is uncomfortable in our ears. "Art inhabits temperate regions," said André Gide in 1940. Well, not always; but if the statement is perhaps a little inaccurate in the range of its generality, we can understand what led Gide to make it, for he goes on: "And doubtless the greatest harm this war is doing to culture is to create a profusion of extreme passions which, by a sort of inflation, brings about a devaluation of all moderate sentiments." And the devaluation of the moderate sentiments brings a concomitant devaluation of the extreme passions: "The dying anguish of Roland or the distress of a Lear stripped of power moves us by its exceptional quality but loses its special eloquence when reproduced simultaneously in several thousand copies." The extreme has become the commonplace of our day. This is not a situation which can be legislated or criticized out of existence, but while it endures we are not in a position to make a proper judgment of Howells, a man of moderate sentiments. It is a disqualification that we cannot regard with complacency, for if Gide is right, it implies that we are in a fair way of being disqualified from making any literary judgments at all.

# The Bostonians

*The Bostonians* is one of a pair of novels, the other being *The Princess Casamassima,* which, in the family of Henry James's works, have a special connection with each other, a particular isolate relationship, as of twins. They were published in the same year, 1886, their previous serial appearances in magazines having been in part concurrent, and although *The Bostonians* was in point of fact the earlier conceived and the first written, they almost seem to have been composed simultaneously, in a single act of creation. They are set apart from James's other novels by having in common a quick responsiveness to the details of the outer world, an explicit awareness of history, of the grosser movements of society and civilization. They share a curious knowledge of the little groups of queer people who, in small dark rooms, agitate the foolish questions which will eventually be decided on the broad field of the future. Very likely it was because James was conscious of these characteristics of the two books—and, we feel, was pleased with them as the evidence of the enlargement of his social intelligence—that he had especially high hopes that the two novels would be happily received by the public.

The disappointment of these hopes is well known. With the

exception of his later defeat in the theater, no check given to James's ambition was so disastrous. The English press treated *The Princess Casamassima* with an almost absolute contempt, and if it was more indulgent with *The Bostonians,* this was only because it found some satisfaction in an American's account of the eccentricity of American manners. The American reviewers were outraged by *The Bostonians;* their more lenient response to *The Princess Casamassima* was in part dictated by their settled opinion of the English social system, which the book might be thought to satirize. Both novels were called queer and foolish, and their failure caused a serious decline in their author's reputation and market.

When, in April of 1883, James had written out in his notebook the full scenario of *The Bostonians,* he had summarized his intention by saying, "I wished to write a very *American* tale." [1] It is possible to say of those of James's novels that are set in America—*The Bostonians* is the last until *The Ivory Tower* of some twenty years later—that they have a tone different from the novels which are set in Europe. I regard with suspicion my natural impulse to say that this is a specifically "American" tone, for I should not know how to explain with any confidence what that is. Yet it seems to me worth observing that, as against the heavy chiaroscuro which in *The Princess Casamassima* is appropriate to the rich clotted past of civilization as that novel evokes it, *The Bostonians* seems suffused by "the dry American light," and that it is marked by a comicality which has rather

[1] The tense of the predicate verb cannot pass without notice. James was not to compose the book until two years later, but when once he had completed the scenario, he felt that the main work was behind him, so natural to him was the act of writing, so little uncertainty intervened for him between the intention and the act. Yet no one who has read both the scenario and the novel can fail to see how much was conceived in the actual writing that could never have been conceived in the scenario, however "divine" James thought "the principle of the scenario" to be.

more kinship with American than with British humor, or with wit of any transatlantic kind. It is said of Miss Birdseye that "she was heroic, she was sublime, the whole moral history of Boston was reflect in her displaced spectacles"; it is said of Dr. Mary Prance that "it is true that if she had been a boy, she would have borne some relation to a girl," and also that "she was determined that she wouldn't be a patient, and it seemed that the only way not to be one was to be a doctor"—humor is latent in all James's writing, implicit in the nature of his prose, but I can bring to mind no other of his novels in which it breaks so gaily out of latency and implicitness into the memorable free overtness of such sentences as these and of scenes analogous to these sentences.

As a representation of the American actuality, *The Bostonians* is in every way remarkable, and its originality is striking. James's Boston, Cambridge, and Cape Cod are superbly rendered, and these localities may still be known—for they have changed less than most American places—through his descriptions of them. No American writer before James had so fully realized the contemporary, physical scene of moral action and social existence. Nor had the nature of the American social existence ever been so brilliantly suggested. Manners have changed since James wrote, but not the peculiar tenuity of the fabric of American social life. The London of *The Princess Casamassima* is no doubt the city of dreadful loneliness, and the barriers of class which it represents are real enough, yet the story sees to it that people at opposite social poles from each other shall meet and become involved with each other. It is thus perfectly in the tradition of the English novel, which characteristically likes the social mixture to be thick and variously composed, and this is a literary preference which corresponds, at whatever distance, to an actuality of English life. But in the America of *The Bostonians,* as in the America that Tocqueville had observed some forty years before, society is but little organized to allow for variousness and complexity, and the social atoms seem to have a centrifugal tendency. Basil Ransom lives in New York with no other companion than his little variety actress. He makes every effort to avoid the company of his cousin, Mrs. Luna, and she, a lady of family and means, seems to have no social circle at all. Mrs. Burrage is by way of being a New York "hostess," but the guests at the party which she gives for Verena Tarrant seem all to have met each other for the first time. It is of the essence of Olive Chancellor's nature that she cannot endure social intercourse; a speech to a crowd is her notion of human communication, and she cannot laugh. Verena Tarrant has presumably never had a friend until Olive Chancellor institutes their ambiguous alliance. Dr. Prance lives in virtual solitude. Miss Birdseye, having devoted a long life to humanity, becomes herself an object of devotion, but rather as if she were everyone's old school, or some dear outworn ideal. The character of Miss Birdseye scandalized Boston because it was thought to be a portrait of Elizabeth Peabody, Hawthorne's famous reforming sister-in-law, and William James—who had, in any case, a poor opinion of *The Bostonians*—undertook to rebuke his brother for his failure of taste. (Henry replied in a letter, a masterpiece of justifiable ambiguity, which has become the classic statement of the relation of the novelist's imagination to real persons.) Even with the most extravagant notions of the Boston genteel sensibility, it is difficult to understand what the ground of the offense was supposed to be, for if Miss Birdseye is indeed a portrait of Miss Peabody, it is the tenderest and most endearing imaginable. And perhaps that is what constituted the offense—for the law recognizes a certain wrong for which the novelist may be liable; it is called "invasion of privacy," and we may suppose that Boston was disturbed because James had committed this wrong, not in the mere legal meaning of the term but in a way far more disturbing: it was not Miss Peabody's privacy that he had invaded but rather the privacy of his readers. He had forced them into intimacy with a person whom they daily greeted, he had made her available to their understanding and to their conscious love, had terribly implied that the actual woman might be the object of the same emotions that they inevitably felt toward the image of her in the novel.

*The Bostonians* and *The Princess Casamassima* seem to be set apart from the rest of James's canon by the public and political matter with which they deal. But their representation of large, overt, opposed forces and principles does not, in point of fact, mark their inspiration as of an essentially different kind from that of James's other novels. It may be said of James—with, of course, some risk of excessive simplification—that virtually all his fiction represents the conflict of two principles, of which one is radical, the other conservative. The two principles are constant, although circumstances change their particular manifestations and the relative values which they are to be judged to have. They may be thought of as energy and inertia; or spirit and matter; or spirit and letter; or force and form; or creation and possession; or Libido and Thanatos. In their simpler manifestations the first term of the grandiose duality is generally regarded with unqualified sympathy and is identified with the ideality of youth, or with truth, or with art, or with America; the second term is regarded with hostility and represented as being one with age, or convention, or philistinism, or decadent Europe. But James's mind is nothing if not "dialectical"—the values assigned to each of the two opposing principles are not permitted to be fixed and constant. Daisy Miller's crude innocent defiance of European conventions is as right as rain, but *Madame de Mauves* suggests that only a small change in circumstance can make American innocence a downright malevolence. Art as against the philistine morality may not always be in the right—creation may corrupt itself into its opposite, possession, as in *The Author of Beltraffio.* Life may be seen to express itself in death and through death. And in *The Birthplace* James seems to be saying that truth can exist only in and through the life of institutions, or that it can be communicated only through sadly inadequate approximations of truth.

The nature of the terms of James's dialectic suggests why his fiction is always momentous. And it is quite within the scope of his genius to infer the political macrocosm from the personal microcosm, to write large and public the disorders of the personal life and to suppose, as he did in *The Bostonians* and *The Princess Casamassima,* that it is the most natural thing in the world that they should

> Divert and crack, rend and deracinate
> The unity and married calm of states. . . .

If we compare the two political movements which James undertook to represent, the revolutionary anarchism of *The Princess Casamassima* will perhaps on first inspection seem to promise more as a theme for a novel than the militant feminism of *The Bostonians.* In a struggle for general social justice there is a natural force and dignity; and in a violent revolutionary intention there is the immediate possibility of high tragedy. But the doctrinaire demand for the equality of the sexes may well seem to promise but a wry and constricted story, a tale of mere eccentricity. The movement for female equality which became endemic in America and in the Protestant countries of Europe in the nineteenth century was predominantly social and legal in its program and even had—although not always—an outright anti-erotic bias which exposed it to the imputation of crankishness and morbidity. It would seem to be susceptible only of comic treatment, and the comedy it seems to propose is not of an attractive kind—it cannot, we know, have anything of the ancient bold freedom of *Lysistrata* or *The Thesmophoriazusae,* in which the women of Athens, in their very act of subverting the natural order of things, affirm the natural erotic community between men and women.

There is indeed some unpleasantness in the comedy of *The Bostonians,* yet exactly by risking this, by daring to seize on the qualities of the women's-rights movement which were "unnatural" and morbid, James possessed himself of a subject which was even larger in its significance than that of *The Princess Casamassima.* A movement of social revolution may question the culture in which it exists, or it may not—indeed we can say of social revolutions that they do not in fact question cultures as much as they seem to do and say they do. But a movement of sexual revolution is to be understood as a question which a culture puts to itself, and right down to its very roots. It is a question about what it means to be a man and what it means to be a woman—about the quality of being which people wish to have. James was interested in the thin vagaries of the female movement of reform only as they suggested a conflict between men and women that went far deeper than any quarrel over rights and equalities. And the conflict that he perceived was not the battle of the sexes which Meredith and Shaw delighted in, a fine formality of marching and countermarching and intricate maneuver on a commodious plain, chosen by mutual consent, the point of the engagement being to demonstrate that women have as bright a spiritedness, as firm a resolution, and as particular an intention of sexuality as men. The opposing forces met on the field as if by appointment, they were animated by the sense of adventure, and defeat brought nothing much worse than honorable captivity on parole—no one in the least believes that John Tanner regrets his surrender to Ann Whitfield. The conflict which James described was very different from this. It was the bitter total war of the sexes which Strindberg conceived and which reached its fullest ideological and artistic expression in the works of D. H. Lawrence.

Tocqueville, whose great book figures in *The Bostonians* because it is the favorite reading of the hero of the novel, had noted the beginnings of sexual disorientation of America; and in James's own time, American observers who were not bound by convention, men so unlike as Walt Whitman and Henry Adams, were aware that something had gone wrong with the sexual life of the nation. "The men hate the women, and the women hate the men," Whitman had said. Adams spoke of American men as having sacrificed their sexuality to business and the machine, and as having induced in American women an indifference even to maternity. And James, when he had set down his intention of "writing a very *American* tale," went on to say, "I asked myself what was the most salient and peculiar point of our social life, the answer was: the situation of women, the decline of the sentiment of sex. . . ."

No more than Tocqueville or Henry Adams or D. H. Lawrence did James understand the sexual situation as an isolated fact, however momentous. For him, as for them, it was the sign of a general diversion of the culture from the course of nature. He makes this plain by his choice of a hero for *The Bostonians*. It was of course essential to his plan that his hero be an outlander, alien to the culture of Boston, and James at first thought that he should be a young man from the West. But a Western hero, he soon saw, was not possible. It must have occurred to him, for one thing, that in the West progressive social and political ideas had established themselves with relative ease, feminism in particular having made far greater advances than in the East, so that he would scarcely be setting up a counterprinciple to Boston. And then the assumptions about a Western hero were inevitably that he was emancipated from tradition, optimistic, concerned with practice rather than with theory, and likely to be impatient of intellectual refinements, and, of course, that he was materially successful. Such a hero might indeed be used to make a cultural-sexual point—in 1906 the Western hero of William Vaughn Moody's *The Great Divide* was to rape the New England heroine for her own good; the audiences of Broadway were delighted with this show of benevolent violence which, as the play made clear, was symbolic of the energies of modern business enterprise and quite disposed of the decadent finickiness of the New England conscience. James had no desire for such an effect. He understood quite as well as Lawrence that the true masculine principle could not be affirmed by a hero who was energetic and successful in the material business of the modern world. In the dramatic nature of the case the spokesman for masculinity should be able to lay claim to none but personal powers; and he will be the better suited to his role if, like Basil Ransom, he has witnessed and participated in the defeat of his cultural tradition, if he has suffered the ruin of his fortunes, and is a stranger in the land of his conquerors.

By choosing a Southerner for his hero, James gained an immediate and immeasurable advantage. By this one stroke he set his story beyond any danger of seeming to be a mere bicker between morbid women and stupid men, the subject of dull, ill-natured jokes. When he involved the feminist movement with even a late adumbration of the immense tragic struggle between North and South, he made it plain that his story had to do with a cultural crisis. Nor could this crisis, if properly understood, seem particular to America, for North and South, as James understands them, represent the two opposing elements in that elaborate politics of culture which, all over the civilized world, has been the great essential subject of the literature of the nineteenth and twentieth centuries.

The South had never had a vigorous intellectual life, and of the systematic apologists for its customs and manners as against the customs and manners of an ever more powerful industrial capitalism, only a very few had been men of real intellectual authority. Yet with the strange previsionary courage which led him, in *The Princess Casamassima,* to imagine types of political character unknown to his own time but familiar to ours, James conceived Basil Ransom as if he were the leading, ideal intelligence of the group of gifted men who, a half-century later, were to rise in the South and to muster in its defense whatever force may be available to an intelligent romantic conservatism. Rejecting much of the sentimental legend of the South, admitting the Southern faults and falsities the more easily because they believed that no civilization can be anything but imperfect, the Southern Agrarians yet said that the South stood for a kind of realism which the North, with its abstract intellectuality, was forgetting to its cost. Like their imagined proto-martyr Ransom, they asserted a distrust of theory, an attachment to tradition, and above all, the tragic awareness of the intractability of the human circumstance.

But Basil Ransom is more daring than any of his intellectual descendants of the South. He has the courage of the collateral British line of romantic conservatives—he is akin to Yeats, Lawrence, and Eliot in that he experiences his cultural fears in the most personal way possible, translating them into sexual fear, the apprehension of the loss of manhood. "The whole generation is womanised," he says, "the masculine tone is passing out of the world; it's a feminine, a nervous, hysterical, chattering, canting age, an age of hollow phrases and false delicacy and exaggerated solicitudes and coddled sensibilities, which, if we don't soon look out, will usher in the reign of mediocrity, of the feeblest and flattest and the most pretentious that has ever been. The masculine character, the ability to dare and endure, to know and yet not to fear reality, to look the world in the face and take it for what it is—a very queer and partly very base mixture—this is what I want to preserve, or rather, as I may say, to recover; and I must say that I don't in the least care what becomes of you ladies while I make the attempt."

And the fear of the loss of manhood, which we are familiar with in Yeats, in Lawrence, and in *The Waste Land,* is given reason for its existence everywhere in *The Bostonians.* The book is full of malign, archaic influences; it is suffused with primitive fear. It is not for nothing that Olive Chancellor's sister is named Mrs. Luna—with her shallow, possessive sexuality, which has the effect of conjuring away all masculine potency, she might as well have been named Mrs. Hecate. The very name of Olive Chancellor might suggest a deteriorated Minerva, presiding in homosexual chastity over the Athens of the New World. The meeting of Olive's colleagues is referred to as a rendezvous of witches on the Brocken, a characterization which is supported throughout the book by James's rather unpleasant sense of the threatening sordidness of almost all women except those in their first youth. Verena Tarrant is conceived as a sort of Iphigenia in Tauris, forced to preside as the priestess of the sacrifice of male captives. Basil Ransom is explicit in his feeling that when he is with Olive Chancellor he is not "safe." And indeed his position is at all times a precarious one. We have the impression that he is the only man in Boston, among hordes of doctrinaire Bacchae, and certainly he is the only man in the book—Verena's poor young suitor, Burrage, lives under the shadow of his mother; Dr. Tarrant is a kind of shaman, gloomily doing sexual service of some dim, grim, shameful kind to deprived Boston ladies; and Matthias Pardon, the newspaper man, is represented as the castrate priest of the huge idol of publicity, which, in the dialectic of the book, stands in hateful opposition to the life of emotion and true sexuality. Perhaps the novel's crucial scene is that which takes place in Memorial Hall at Harvard, when Ransom finds it necessary to enforce upon Verena's imagination the pathos of the fate of the young men who had died in the recent war. These young men had been his enemies, but he feels bound to them by the ties of the sex they have in common, and the danger of battle had never been so great as the sexual danger of his present civil situation.

There is one biographical circumstance of the writing of *The Bostonians* which ought to be mentioned in any account of the novel. I have no doubt that it bears in an important way upon the personal problems of Henry James's own life which are implied, we must inevitably suppose, by Ransom's fears. But the investigation of these problems lies outside my competence and my purpose, and I mention the circumstance only for reasons that are purely literary, only, that is, because an awareness of it is likely to make for a warmer understanding of the book.

In 1881 James visited his country and his family for the first time since 1876, the year in which he had made his decision to establish his home in England. From the beginning the visit was not a happy one. James disliked Boston, where he lived to be near his parents in Cambridge, and he was bored and restless. In January he went to stay with Henry Adams in Washington, and there, on the thirtieth of the month, he received the telegram announcing his mother's serious illness which was intended to prepare him for her death.

It was James's first familial loss and it shocked and saddened him deeply. Yet it also, as he writes of it in his notebook, moved him to a kind of joy. He had always known that he loved his mother, but not until he saw her in her shroud did he know how tender his love was. Mrs. James had been a quiet woman, with none of the spirited quality of her husband, the elder Henry James. But her son wrote of her, "She was our life, she was the house, she was the keystone of the arch. She held us all together, and without her we are scattered reeds. She was patience, she was wisdom, she was exquisite maternity." And as his impassioned memorial of her draws to its close, he says, "It was the perfect mother's life—the life of a perfect wife. To bring her children into the world—to expend herself, for years, for their happiness and welfare—then, when they had reached a full maturity and were absorbed in the world and their own interests —to lay herself down in her ebbing strength and yield up her pure soul to the celestial power that had given her this divine commission." Perhaps nothing that Henry James ever wrote approaches this passage in the explicit cognizance it takes of the biological nature of moral fact.

James stayed with his father and his sister Alice until May, when, at his father's insistence, he returned to England and his work. But in December came the news of his father's imminent death. The elder Henry James, it was said, had no wish to survive his wife; in his last illness he refused food and gently faded away. The younger Henry arrived too late to see his father for the last time, too late even for the funeral. William James's famous letter of farewell to their "sacred old Father" also arrived too late, but Henry took it to the Cambridge cemetery and read it aloud over the grave, sure, as he wrote to William, that "somewhere out of the depths of the still bright winter air" the father heard.

His mother was the strength that is not power as the world knows **power, the** strength of conservation, the unseen, unregarded, seemingly unexerted force that holds things to their center. She had lived the ancient elemental course of life, which is without theory or formulation, too certain of itself and too much at one with itself even to aspire. His father, according to his particular lights, had had the masculine power, "the ability to dare and endure, to know and yet not to fear reality." During his sad visit to his parental land in 1883, the last for twenty years, when the parental family had come to an end, Henry James wrote out the scenario of *The Bostonians,* which is a story of the parental house divided against itself, of the keystone falling from the arch, of the sacred mothers refusing their commission and the sacred fathers endangered.

# Wordsworth and the Rabbis

OUR COMMEMORATION of the hundredth anniversary of Wordsworth's death must inevitably be charged with the consciousness that if Wordsworth were not kept in mind by the universities he would scarcely be remembered at all.[1] In our culture it is not the common habit to read the books of a century ago, and very likely all that we can mean when we say that a writer of the past is "alive" in people's minds is that, to those who once read him as a college assignment or who have formed an image of him from what they have heard about him, he exists as an attractive idea, as an intellectual possibility. And if we think of the three poets whom Matthew Arnold celebrated in his "Memorial Verses," we know that Byron is still attractive and possible, and so is Goethe. But Wordworth is not attractive and not an intellectual possibility. He was once the great, the speaking poet for all who read English. He spoke both to the ordinary reader and to the literary man. But now the literary man outside the university will scarcely think of referring to Wordsworth as one of the important events of modern literature; and to the ordinary reader he is likely to exist as the very

[1] The Centenary was celebrated in America at Cornell and Princeton Universities on April 21 and 22, 1950.

type of the poet whom life has passed by, presumably for the good reason that he passed life by.

If we ask why Wordsworth is no longer the loved poet he once was, why, indeed, he is often thought to be rather absurd and even a little despicable, one answer that suggests itself is that for modern taste he is too Christian a poet. He is certainly not to be wholly characterized by the Christian element of his poetry. Nor can we say of him that he is a Christian poet in the same sense that Dante is, or Donne, or Hopkins. With them the specific Christian feeling and doctrine is of the essence of their matter and their conscious intention, as it is not with Wordsworth. Yet at the present time, the doctrinal tendency of the world at large being what it is, that which *is* Christian in Wordsworth may well seem to be more prominent than it ever was before, and more decisive. I have in mind his concern for the life of humbleness and quiet, his search for peace, his sense of the burdens of this life, those which are inherent in the flesh and spirit of man. Then there is his belief that the bonds of society ought to be inner and habitual, not merely external and formal, and that the strengthening of these bonds by the acts and attitudes of charity is a great and charming duty. Christian too seems his responsiveness to the idea that there is virtue in the discharge of duties which are of the great world and there- fore dangerous to simple peace—his sense of affinity with Milton was as much with Milton's political as with his poetical career, and the Happy Warrior is the man who has, as it were, sacrificed the virtuous peace of the poet to the necessities of public life. There is his impulse to submit to the conditions of life under a guidance that is at once certain and mysterious; his sense of the possibility and actuality of enlightenment, it need scarcely be said, is one of the characteristic things about him. It was not he who said that the world was a vale of soul-making, but the poet who did make this striking paraphrase of the Christian sentiment could not have uttered it had not Wordsworth made it possible for him to do so.[2] And then, above all, there is his consciousness of the *neighbor,* his impulse to bring into the circle of significant life those of the neighbors who are simple and outside the circle of social pride, and also those who in the judgment of the world are queer and strange and useless: faith and hope were to him very great virtues, but he conceived that they rested upon the still greater virtue, charity.

Certainly what I have called Christian in Wordsworth scarcely approaches, let alone makes up, the sum of Christianity. But then no personal document or canon can do that, not even the work of a poet who is specifically Christian in the way of Dante, or of Donne, or of Hopkins. When we speak of a poet as being of a particular religion, we do not imply in him completeness or orthodoxy, or even explicitness of doctrine, but only that his secular utterance has the decisive mark of the religion upon it. And if a religion is manifold in its aspects and extensive in time, the marks that are to be found on the poets who are in a relation to it will be various in kind. It seems to me that the marks of Christianity on Wordsworth are clear and indelible. It is therefore worth trying the hypothesis that the world today does not like him because it does not like the Christian quality and virtues.

But the question at once arises whether this hypothesis is actually available to us. Professor Hoxie Neal Fairchild says that it is not. In the chapter on Wordsworth in the third volume of his *Religious Trends in English Poetry,* he tells us that Wordsworth was *not* a Christian poet and goes on to express his doubt that Wordsworth was ever properly to be

---

[2] It is of some relevance to our argument that when Keats wrote the famous phrase he believed that he was controverting, not affirming, a tendency of Christian thought.

called a Christian person even when he became a communicant of the Church and its defender. And Professor Fairchild goes so far as to tell us that as a poet Wordsworth is actually dangerous to the Christian faith. He is dangerous in the degree that he may be called religious at all, for his religion is said to be mere religiosity, the religion of nothing more than the religious emotion, beginning and ending in the mere sense of transcendence. Naked of dogma, bare of precise predication of God and the nature of man, this religiosity of Wordsworth's is to be understood as a pretentious and seductive rival of Christianity. It is the more dangerous because it gives license to man's pretensions—Professor Fairchild subscribes to the belief that romanticism must bear a large part of the responsibility for our present ills, especially for those which involve man's direct and conscious inhumanity to man.

We can surely admit the cogency of Professor Fairchild's argument within the terms of its intention. The nineteenth century was in many respects a very Christian century, but in the aspect of it which bulks largest in our minds it developed chiefly the ethical and social aspects of Christian belief, no doubt at the cost of the dogmatic aspect, which had already been weakened by the latitudinarian tendency of the eighteenth century. And it is probably true that when the dogmatic principle in religion is slighted, religion goes along for a while on generalized emotion and ethical intention—"morality touched by emotion"—and then loses the force of its impulse, even the essence of its being. In this sort of attenuation of religion, romanticism in general, and Wordsworth in particular, did indeed play a part by making the sense of transcendence and immanence so real and so attractive. During the most interesting and important period of his career, Wordsworth seems to have been scarcely aware of the doctrines of the Church in which he had

been reared. He spoke of faith, hope, and charity without reference to the specifically Christian source and end of these virtues.
His sense of the need for salvation did not take the least account of the Christian means of salvation. Of evil in the Christian sense of the word, of sin as an element of the nature of man,
he also took no account.

And yet, all this being true, as we look at Wordsworth in
the context of his own time and in the context of our time, what
may properly be called the Christian element of his poetry can
be made to speak to us, as it spoke to so many Christians in the
nineteenth century, as it spoke to so many who were not Christians and made them in one degree or another accessible to
Christianity.

"Any religious movement," says Christopher Dawson, an orthodox Christian scholar, "which adopts a purely critical and
negative attitude to culture is . . . a force of destruction and
disintegration which mobilizes against it the healthiest and most
constructive elements in society—elements which can by no
means be dismissed as worthless from the religious point of
view." Romanticism in general was far from worthless to Christianity, far from worthless to that very Anglo-Catholicism which
inclines to be so strict with it. And this is true of Wordsworth in
particular. He certainly did not in his great period accept as
adequate what the Church taught about the nature of man. But
he was one of the few poets who really discovered something
about the nature of man. What he discovered can perhaps be
shown, if the argument be conducted by a comparison of for-
mulas and doctrine, to be at variance with the teachings of
Christianity. Yet I think it can also be shown that Wordsworth
discovered much that a strong Christianity must take account
of, and be easy with, and make use of. It can be shown too, I

believe, that the Church has found advantage in what Wordsworth has told us of the nature of man.

Professor Fairchild, I need scarcely say, understands Christianity far better than I do, through his having studied it ever so much more than I have; and of course he understands it far better than I might ever hope to, because he has experienced it as a communicant. He has also, I am sure, tested his conclusions by the whole tendency of the Church to which he gives so strong and thoughtful an allegiance. My own reading of this tendency, at least as it appears in literature and in literary criticism, where it has been so influential, is that it is not inclined to accept Wordsworth as a Christian poet. And still, even against the force of Professor Fairchild's judgment, I cannot help feeling that there is an important element of Christianity with which Wordsworth has a significant affinity, even though this element is not at the present time of chief importance to Christian intellectuals.

But this is not an occasion for anything like contentiousness, and I ought not to seem to be forcing even a great poet into a faith whose members do not want him there. I am not, in any case, so much concerned to prove that Wordsworth is a Christian poet as to account for a certain quality in him which makes him unacceptable to the modern world. And so, without repudiating my first hypothesis, I shall abandon it for this fresh one: that the quality in Wordsworth that now makes him unacceptable is a Judaic quality.

My knowledge of the Jewish tradition is, I fear, all too slight to permit me to hope that I can develop this new hypothesis in any very enlightening way. Yet there is one Jewish work of traditional importance which I happen to know with some intimacy, and it lends a certain color of accuracy to my notion.

This is the work called *Pirke Aboth,* that is, the sayings, the *sententiae,* of the Fathers. It was edited in the second century of the present era by the scholar and teacher who bore the magnificent name of Rabbi Jehudah the Prince, and who is traditionally referred to by the even more magnificent name of *Rabbi* —that is to say, *the* rabbi, the master teacher, the greatest of all. In its first intention *Pirke Aboth,* under the name *Aboth,* "Fathers," was one of the tractates of the Mishnah, which is the traditional Jewish doctrine represented chiefly by rabbinical decisions. But *Aboth* itself, the last of the tractates, does not deal with decisions; nor is it what a common English rendering of the longer title, "Ethics of the Fathers," would seem to imply, for it is not a system of ethics at all but simply a collection of maxims and *pensées,* some of them very fine and some of them very dull, which praise the life of study and give advice on how to live it.

In speaking of Wordsworth a recollection of boyhood cannot be amiss—my intimacy with *Pirke Aboth* comes from my having read it many times in boyhood. It certainly is not the kind of book a boy is easily drawn to read, and certainly I did not read it out of piety. On the contrary, indeed: for when I was supposed to be reading my prayers—very long, and in the Hebrew language, which I never mastered—I spent the required time and made it seem that I was doing my duty by reading the English translation of the *Pirke Aboth,* which, although it is not a devotional work, had long ago been thought of as an aid to devotion and included in the prayer book. It was more attractive to me than psalms, meditations, and supplications; it seemed more humane, and the Fathers had a curious substantiality. Just where they lived I did not know, nor just when, and certainly the rule of life they recommended had a very quaint difference from the life I knew, or, indeed, from any life that I wanted to know.

Yet they were real, their way of life had the charm of coherence. And when I went back to them, using R. Travers Herford's scholarly edition and translation of their sayings,[3] I could entertain the notion that my early illicit intimacy with them had had its part in preparing the way for my responsiveness to Wordsworth, that between the Rabbis and Wordsworth an affinity existed.

But I must at once admit that a large difficulty stands in the way of the affinity I suggest. The *Aboth* is a collection of the sayings of masters of the written word. The ethical life it recommends has study as both its means and its end, the study of Torah, of the Law, which alone can give blessedness. So that from the start I am at the disadvantage of trying to make a conjunction between scholars living for the perpetual interpretation of a text and a poet for whom the natural world was at the heart of his doctrine and for whom books were barren leaves. The Rabbis expressed a suspiciousness of the natural world which was as extreme as Wordsworth's suspiciousness of study. That the warning was given at all seems to hint that it was possible for the Rabbis to experience the natural world as a charm and a temptation: still, the *Aboth* does warn us that whoever interrupts his study to observe the beauty of a fine tree or a fine meadow is guilty of sin. And yet I think it can be said without more extravagance than marks my whole comparison that it is precisely here, where they seem most to differ, that the Rabbis and Wordsworth are most at one. For between the Law as the Rabbis understood it and Nature as Wordsworth understood that, there is a pregnant similarity.

[3] *Pirke Aboth,* edited with introduction, translation and commentary, third edition (New York: 1945). I have also consulted the edition and translation of the Very Rev. Dr. Joseph H. Hertz, Chief Rabbi of the British Empire, and in my quotations I have drawn upon both versions, and sometimes, when it suited my point, I have combined two versions in a single quotation.

The Rabbis of the *Aboth* were Pharisees. I shall assume that
the long scholarly efforts of Mr. Herford, as well as those of
George Foot Moore, have by now made it generally known that
the Pharisees were not in actual fact what tradition represents
them to have been. They were anything but mere formalists, and
of course they were not the hypocrites of popular conception.
Here is Mr. Herford's statement of the defining principle of
Pharisaism: "The central conception of Pharisaism is Torah, the
divine Teaching, the full and inexhaustible revelation which
God had made. The knowledge of what was revealed was to be
sought, and would be found, in the first instance in the written
text of the Pentateuch; but the revelation, the real Torah, was the
meaning of what was there written, the meaning as interpreted
by all the recognized and accepted methods of the schools, and
unfolded in ever greater fullness of detail by successive generations of devoted teachers. The written text of the Pentateuch
might be compared to the mouth of a well; the Torah was the
water which was drawn from it. He who wished to draw the
water must needs go to the well, but there was no limit to
the water which was there for him to draw. . . . The study of
Torah . . . means therefore much more than the study of the
Pentateuch, or even of the whole Scripture, regarded as mere
literature, written documents. It means the study of the revelation made through those documents, the divine teaching therein
imparted, the divine thought therein disclosed. Apart from the
direct intercourse of prayer, the study of Torah was the way
of closest approach to God; it might be called the Pharisaic
form of the Beatific Vision. To study Torah was, to the devout
Pharisee, to 'think God's thoughts after him,' as Kepler said."
The Rabbis, that is, found sermons in texts, tongues in the
running commentary.

And Mr. Herford goes on to say that it might be observed of

the *Aboth* that it makes very few direct references to God. "This is true," he says, "but it is beside the mark. Wherever Torah is mentioned, there God is implied. He is behind the Torah, the Revealer of what is Revealed."

What I am trying to suggest is that, different as the immediately present objects were in each case, Torah for the Rabbis, Nature for Wordsworth, there existed for the Rabbis and for Wordsworth a great object, which is from God and might be said to represent Him as a sort of surrogate, a divine object to which one can be in an intimate passionate relationship, an active relationship—for Wordsworth's "wise passiveness" is of course an activity—which one can, as it were, handle, and in a sense create, drawing from it inexhaustible meaning by desire, intuition, and attention.

And when we turn to the particulars of the *Aboth* we see that the affinity continues. In Jewish tradition the great Hillel has a peculiarly Wordsworthian personality, being the type of gentleness and peace, and having about him a kind of *joy* which has always been found wonderfully attractive; and Hillel said—was, indeed, in the habit of saying: he "used to say"—"If I am not for myself, who, then, is for me? And if I am for myself, what then am I?" Mr. Herford implies that this is a difficult utterance. But it is not difficult for the reader of Wordsworth, who finds the Wordsworthian moral essence here, the interplay between individualism and the sense of community, between an awareness of the self that must be saved and developed, and an awareness that the self is yet fulfilled only in community.

Then there is this saying of Akiba's: "All is foreseen, and yet free will is given; and the world is judged by grace, and yet all is according to the work." With how handsome a boldness it handles the problem of fate and free will, or "grace" and "works," handles the problem by stating it as an antinomy, escaping the woeful claustral preoccupation with the alternatives, but not their grandeur. This refusal to be fixed either in fate or in free will, either in grace or in works, and the recognition of both, are characteristic of Wordsworth.

There are other parallels to be drawn. For example, one finds in the *Aboth* certain remarks which have a notable wit and daring because they go against the whole tendency of the work in telling us that the multiplication of words is an occasion for sin, and the chief thing is not study but action. One finds the injunction to the scholar to divide his time between study and a trade, presumably in the interest of humility. And the scholar is warned that the world must not be too much with him, that, getting and spending, he lays waste his powers. There is the concern, so typical of Wordsworth, with the "ages of man," with the right time in the individual's development for each of life's activities. But it is needless to multiply the details of the affinity, which in any case must not be insisted on too far. All that I want to suggest is the community of ideal and sensibility between the *Aboth* and the canon of Wordsworth's work—the passionate contemplation and experience of the great object which is proximate to Deity; then the plain living that goes with the high thinking, the desire for the humble life and the discharge of duty; and last, but not least important, a certain insouciant acquiescence in the anomalies of the moral order of the universe, a respectful indifference to, or graceful surrender before, the mysteries of the moral relation of God to man.

This last element, as it is expressed in the *pensée* of Akiba which I have quoted, has its connection with something in the *Aboth* which for me is definitive of its quality. Actually it is something not in the *Aboth* but left out—we find in the tractate no implication of moral struggle. We find the energy of assiduity but not the energy of resistance. We hear about sin, but we do not hear of the sinful nature of man. Man in the *Aboth* guards against sin but he does not struggle against it, and of evil we hear nothing at all.

When we have observed this, it is natural to observe next that there is no mention in the *Aboth* of courage or heroism. In our culture we connect the notion of courage or heroism with the religious life. We conceive of the perpetual enemy within and the perpetual enemy without, which must be "withstood," "overcome," "conquered"—the language of religion and the language of fighting are in our culture assimilated to each other. Not so in the *Aboth*. The enemy within seems not to be conceived of at all. The enemy without is never mentioned, although the *Aboth* was compiled after the Dispersion, after the Temple and the nation had been destroyed—with what heroism in the face of suffering we know from Josephus. Of the men whose words are cited in the *Aboth,* many met martyrdom for their religion, and the martyrology records their calm and fortitude in torture and death; of Akiba it records his heroic joy. And yet in their maxims they never speak of courage. There is not a word to suggest that the life of virtue and religious devotion requires the heroic quality.

As much as anything else in my boyhood experience of the *Aboth* it was this that fascinated me. It also repelled me. It had this double effect because it went so clearly against the militancy of spirit which in our culture is normally assumed. And even now, as I consider this indifference to heroism of the *Aboth*, I have the old ambiguous response to it, so that I think I can understand the feelings that readers have when they encounter something similar in Wordsworth. It is what Matthew Arnold noted when in the "Memorial Verses" he compared Wordsworth with Byron, who was for Arnold the embodiment of

militancy of spirit. Arnold said of Wordsworth that part of his
peculiar value to us arose from his indifference to "man's fiery
might," to the Byronic courage in fronting human destiny.

> The cloud of mortal destiny,
> Others will front it fearlessly—
> But who, like him, will put it by?

Arnold certainly did not mean that Wordsworth lacked courage or took no account of it. Wordsworth liked nothing better,
indeed, than to recite examples of courage, but the Wordsworthian courage is different in kind from the Byronic. For one thing,
it is never aware of itself, it is scarcely personal. It is the courage
of mute, insensate things, and it is often associated with such
things, "with rocks, and stones, and trees," or with stars. Michael
on his hilltop, whose character is defined by the light of his
cottage, which was called "The Evening Star," and by the stones
of his sheepfold; or the Leech Gatherer, who is like some old,
great rock; or Margaret, who, like a tree, endured as long as she
might after she was blasted—of the Lesser Celandine it is said
that its fortitude in meeting the rage of the storm is neither its
courage nor its choice but "its necessity in being old," and the
same thing is to be said of all Wordsworth's exemplars of courage: they endure because they are what they are, and we might
almost say that they survive out of a kind of biological faith,
which is not the less human because it is nearly an animal or
vegetable faith; and, indeed, as I have suggested, it is sometimes
nearly mineral. Even the Happy Warrior, the man in arms,
derives his courage not from his militancy of spirit but from
his calm submission to the law of things.

In Wordsworth's vision of life, then, the element of quietude
approaches passivity, even insentience, and the dizzy raptures
of youth have their issue in the elemental existence of which I

have spoken. The scholars of the *Aboth* certainly had no such notion; they lived for intellectual sentience. But where the scholars and Wordsworth are at one is in the quietism, which is not in the least a negation of life, but, on the contrary, an affirmation of life so complete that it needed no saying. To the Rabbis, as I read them, there life was, unquestionable because committed to a divine object. There life was—in our view rather stuffy and airless, or circumscribed and thin, but very intense and absolutely and utterly real, not needing to be affirmed by force or assertion, real because the object of its regard was unquestioned, and because the object was unquestionably more important than the individual person who regarded it and lived by it. To Wordsworth, as I read him, a similar thing was true in its own way. Much as he loved to affirm the dizzy raptures of sentience, of the ear and the eye and the mind, he also loved to move down the scale of being, to say that when the sentient spirit was sealed by slumber, when it was without motion and force, when it was like a rock or a stone or a tree, not hearing or seeing, and passive in the cosmic motion—that even then, perhaps especially then, existence was blessed.

Nothing could be further from the tendency of our Western culture, which is committed to an idea of consciousness and activity, of motion and force. With us the basis of spiritual prestige is some form of aggressive action directed outward upon the world, or inward upon ourselves. During the last century and a half this ideal has been especially strong in literature. If the religious personality of preceding times took to itself certain of the marks of military prestige, the literary personality now takes to itself certain of the marks of religious prestige, in particular the capacity for militant suffering.

A peculiarly relevant example of this lies to hand in T. S. Eliot's explanation of the decline of Wordsworth's genius from its greatness to what Mr. Eliot calls the "still sad music of infirmity." The small joke, so little characteristic of Mr. Eliot's humor, suggests something of the hostile uneasiness that Wordsworth can arouse in us. And Mr. Eliot's theory of the decline suggests the depth of our belief in the value of militancy, of militant suffering, for Mr. Eliot tells us that the trouble with Wordsworth was that he didn't have an eagle: it is that eagle which André Gide's Prometheus said was necessary for success in the spiritual or poetic life—"Il faut avoir un aigle." As an explanation of Wordsworth's poetic career this is, we perceive, merely a change rung on the weary idea that Wordsworth destroyed his poetic genius by reversing his position on the French Revolution or by terminating his connection with Annette Vallon. Wordsworth had no need of an eagle for his greatness, and its presence or absence had nothing to do with the decline of his genius. His pain, when he suffered, was not of the kind that eagles inflict, and his power did not have its source in his pain. But we are disturbed by the absence of the validating, the poetically respectable bird, that aigle obligatoire. We like the fiercer animals. Nothing is better established in our literary life than the knowledge that the tigers of wrath are to be preferred to the horses of instruction, a striking remark which is indeed sometimes very true, although not always. We know that we ought to prefer the bulls in the ring to the horses, and when we choose between the two kinds of horses of Plato's chariot we all know that Plato was wrong, that it is the blacks, not the whites, which are to be preferred. We do not, to be sure, live in the fashion of the beasts we admire in our literary lives, but we cherish them as representing something that we all seek. They are the emblems of the charisma—to borrow from the sociologists a word they have borrowed from the theologians—which is the hot, direct relationship with Godhead, or with the sources of life, upon which depend our notions of what I have called spiritual prestige.

The predilection for the powerful, the fierce, the assertive, the personally militant, is very strong in our culture. We find it in the liberal-bourgeois admiration of the novels of Thomas Wolfe and Theodore Dreiser. On a lower intellectual level we find it in the long popularity of that curious underground work *The Fountainhead*. On a higher intellectual level we find it in certain aspects of the work of Yeats and Lawrence. We find it too, if not in our religion itself, then at least in one of our dominant conceptions of religion—to many intellectuals the violence of Dostoevski represents the natural form of the religious life, to many gentle spirits the ferocity of Léon Bloy seems quite appropriate to the way of faith; and although some years ago Mr. Eliot reprobated D. H. Lawrence, in the name of religion, for his addiction to this characteristic violence, yet for Mr. Eliot the equally violent Baudelaire is pre-eminently a Christian poet.[4]

I cannot give a better description of the quality of our literature with which I am concerned than by quoting the characterization of it which Richard Chase found occasion to make in the course of a review of a work on the nineteenth century by a notable English scholar, Professor Basil Willey. It is relevant to remark that Professor Willey deals with the nineteenth century from the point of view of the Anglican form of Christianity, and Mr. Chase is commenting on Professor Willey's hostility to a certain Victorian figure who, in any discussion of Wordsworth, must inevitably be in our minds—John Stuart Mill. His name seems very queer and shocking when it is spoken together

[4] In his brief introduction to Father Tiverton's *D. H. Lawrence and Human Existence*, Mr. Eliot has indicated that he has changed his mind about Lawrence's relation to the religious life. I think he was right to do so. The revision of his opinion confirms, if anything, what I say of the place of violence in our conception of the religious life.

with the names of the great figures of modern literature. Yet Mr. Chase is right when he says that "among the Victorians, it is Mill who tests the modern mind," and goes on to say that "in relation to him at least two of its weaknesses come quickly to light. The first is its morose desire for dogmatic certainty. The second is its hyperaesthesia: its feeling that no thought is permissible except an extreme thought: that every idea must be directly emblematic of concentration camps, alienation, madness, hell, history, and God; that every word must bristle and explode with the magic potency of our plight."

I must be careful not to seem to speak, as certainly Mr. Chase is not speaking, against the sense of urgency or immediacy, or against power or passion. Nor would I be taken to mean that the Wordsworthian quietism I have described is the whole desideratum of the emotional life. It obviously wasn't that for Wordsworth himself—he may be said to be the first poet who praised movement and speed for their own sakes, and dizziness and danger; he is the poet of rapture. No one can read Book Five of *The Prelude* and remain unaware of Wordsworth's conception of literature as urgency and immediacy, as power and passion. Book Five, which is about literature and the place of reading in our spiritual development, opens with an impressive eschatological vision, a vision of final events—Wordsworth shared in his own way our present sense of the possible end of man and of all the works of man's spirit, and it is important to observe that in the great dream of the Arab who hastens before the advancing flood to rescue Science and Poetry, represented by the Stone and the Shell he carries, the prophecy of the world destroyed is made to seem the expression of the very essence of literature. It is in this book that Wordsworth defends the violence and fearfulness of literature from the "progressive" ideas of his day; it is here that he speaks of the poet as "crazed/By love and feeling, and internal thought/Protracted among endless solitude," and of the "reason" that lies couched "in the blind and awful lair" of the poet's madness; and it is here that he defends the "maniac's" dedication at the cost of the domestic affections:

> Enow there are on earth to take in charge
> Their wives, their children, and their virgin loves,
> Or whatsoever else the heart holds dear;
> Enow to stir for these. . . .

As we speak of Wordsworth's quietism this opposite element of his poetry must be borne in mind. Then too, if we speak in anything like praise of his quietism, we must be conscious of the connection of his quietism with an aspect of his poetry that we rightly dread. When, in *The Excursion,* the Wanderer and the Poet and the Pastor sit upon the gravestones and tell sad stories of the deaths of other mild old men, for the benefit of the Solitary, who has had his fling at life and is understandably a little bitter, we know that something wrong is being done to us; we long for the winding of a horn or the drawing of a sword; we want someone to dash in on a horse—I think we want exactly a stallion, St. Mawr or another; for there can be no doubt about it, Wordsworth, at the extreme or perversion of himself, carries the element of quietude to the point of the denial of sexuality. And this is what makes the *Aboth* eventually seem to us quaint and oppressive, what, I suppose, makes a modern reader uneasy under any of the philosophies which urge us to the contemplative accord with a unitary reality and warn us that the accord will infallibly be disturbed and destroyed by the desires. Whether it be the Torah of the Rabbis, or the Cosmos of Marcus Aurelius, or the Nature of Spinoza or of Wordsworth, the accord with the unitary reality seems to depend upon the suppression not only of the sexual emotions but also of the qualities that are associated with sexuality: high-heartedness, wit, creative innovation, will.

But now, when we have touched upon the Wordsworthian quality that is very close to the Stoic *apatheia,* to not-feeling, let us remember what great particular thing Wordsworth is said to have accomplished. Matthew Arnold said that in a wintry clime, in an iron time, Wordsworth taught us to *feel.* This statement, extreme as it is, will be seen to be not inaccurate if we bring to mind the many instances of spiritual and psychological crisis in the nineteenth century in which affectlessness, the loss of the power to feel, played an important part. *Ennui, noia*—how often we meet with them in nineteenth-century biography; and the *acedia* which was once a disorder of the specifically religious life becomes now a commonplace of secular spirituality. Arnold, when he wrote the "Memorial Verses," could not, of course, have read Mill's autobiography, which so specifically and eloquently confirms Arnold's attribution to Wordsworth of a "healing power" through an ability to make us feel. And yet, although Arnold's statement is accurate so far as it goes, and is supported by Wordsworth's own sense of the overarching intention of his poetic enterprise, it does not go far enough. Wordsworth did, or tried to do, more than make us feel: he undertook to teach us how to *be.*

In *The Prelude,* in Book Two, Wordsworth speaks of a particular emotion which he calls "the sentiment of Being." The "sentiment" has been described in this way: "There is, in sanest hours, a consciousness, a thought that rises, independent, lifted out from all else, calm, like the stars, shining eternal. This is the thought of identity—yours for you, whoever you are, as mine for me. Miracle of miracles, beyond statement, most spiritual and vaguest of earth's dreams, yet hardest basic fact, and only entrance to all facts." This, of course, is not Wordsworth, it is Walt Whitman, but I quote Whitman's statement in exposition of Wordsworth's "sentiment of Being" because it is in some respects rather more boldly explicit, although not necessarily better, than anything that Wordsworth himself wrote about the sentiment, and because Whitman goes on to speak of his "hardest basic fact" as a political fact, as the basis, and the criterion, of democracy.

Through all his poetic life Wordsworth was preoccupied by the idea, by the sentiment, by the problem, of being. All experience, all emotions lead to it. He was haunted by the mysterious fact that he existed. He could discover in himself different intensities and qualities of being—"Tintern Abbey" is the attempt to distinguish these intensities and qualities. Being is sometimes animal; sometimes it is an "appetite and a passion"; sometimes it is almost a suspension of the movement of the breath and blood. The *Lyrical Ballads* have many intentions, but one of the chief of them is the investigation of the problems of being. "We are Seven," which is always under the imputation of bathos, is established in its true nature when we read it as an ontological poem; its subject is the question, What does it mean when we say a person *is*? "The Idiot Boy," which I believe to be a great and not a foolish poem, is a kind of comic assertion of the actuality—and, indeed, the peculiar intensity—of being in a person who is outside the range of anything but our merely mechanical understanding. Johnny on the little horse, flourishing his branch of holly under the moon, is a creature of rapture, who, if he is not quite "human," is certainly elemental, magical,

perhaps a little divine—"It was Johnny, Johnny everywhere."
As much as anyone, and more than many—more than most—
he *is,* and feels that he is.

From even the little I have said, it will be seen that as soon as
the "sentiment of Being" is named, or represented, there arises
a question of its degree of actuality or of its survival. "The glad
animal movements" of the boy, the "appetite" and the "passion"
of the young man's response to Nature easily confirm the sense
of being. So do those experiences which are represented as a
"sleep" or "slumber," when the bodily senses are in abeyance.
But as the man grows older the stimuli to the experience of the
sentiment of being grow fewer or grow less intense—it is this
fact rather than any question of poetic creation (such as troubled
Coleridge) that makes the matter of the Immortality Ode.
Wordsworth, as it were, puts the awareness of being to the test
in situations where its presence may perhaps most easily be
questioned—in very old people. Other kinds of people also
serve for the test, such as idiots, the insane, children, the dead,
but I emphasize the very old because Wordsworth gave particular attention to them, and because we can all be aware from our
own experience what a strain very old people put upon our
powers of attributing to them personal being, "identity." Wordsworth's usual way is to represent the old man as being below the
human condition, apparently scarcely able to communicate, and
then suddenly, startlingly, in what we have learned to call an
"epiphany," to show forth the intensity of his human existence.
The old man in "Animal Tranquillity and Decay" is described
as being so old and so nearly inanimate that the birds regard
him as little as if he were a stone or a tree; for this, indeed, he is
admired, and the poem says that his unfelt peace is so perfect
that it is envied by the very young. He is questioned about his
destination on the road—

> I asked him whither he was bound, and what
> The object of his journey; he replied,
> "Sir! I am going many miles to take
> A last leave of my son, a mariner,
> Who from a sea-fight has been brought to Falmouth,
> And there is dying in an hospital."

The revelation of the actuality of his being, of his humanness, quite dazzles us.[5]

The social and political implication of Wordsworth's preoccupation with ontology is obvious enough. It is not, however, quite what Wordsworth sometimes says it is. The direct political lesson that the poet draws from the Old Cumberland Beggar is interesting, but it is beside his real, his essential, point. "Deem not this man useless," he says in his apostrophe to the political theorists who have it in mind to put the Beggar into a workhouse, and he represents the usefulness of the Beggar as consisting in his serving as the object of a habitual charity and thus as a kind of communal institution, a communal bond. But this demonstrated utility of the Beggar is really secondary to the fact that he *is*—he is a person, he takes a pleasure, even though a minimal one, in his being, and therefore he may not in conscience be dealt with as a mere social unit. So with all the dramatis personae of the *Lyrical Ballads*—the intention of the poet is to require us to acknowledge their being and thus to bring them within the range of conscience, and of something more immediate than conscience, natural sympathy. It is an attractive thing about Wordsworth, and it should be a reassuring thing, that his acute sense of the being of others derives from, and serves to affirm and heighten, his acute sense of his own being.

[5] The concluding lines of the poem as originally printed in *Lyrical Ballads,* where the poem bears the title "Old Man Travelling," were deleted by Wordsworth in subsequent editions, which is a misfortune.

I have spoken of Wordsworth's preoccupation with being as if it were unique, and as if it accounted for, or led to what accounts for, the contemporary alienation from his work and his personality. In some ways his preoccupation *is* unique, and certain aspects of it do lead to the present alienation from him. Yet from what I have said about him, it must be clear that between Wordsworth and the great figures of our literature there is a very close affinity indeed, if only in the one regard of the preoccupation with being. There is scarcely a great writer of our own day who has not addressed himself to the ontological crisis, who has not conceived of life as a struggle to be—not to live, but to be. They do so, to be sure, under a necessity rather different from Wordsworth's, and this necessity makes it seem appropriate that, with Byron, they assert "man's fiery might." (Blake suggests more aptly than Byron the quality of the militancy of most modern writers, but I stay with the terms of the opposition as Arnold gives them to us.) They feel the necessity to affirm the personal qualities that are associated with a former time, presumably a freer and more personally privileged time —they wish, as a character in one of Yeats's plays says, "to bring back the old disturbed exalted life, the old splendor." Their image of freedom and personal privilege is often associated with violence, sometimes of a kind that does not always command the ready assent we are habituated to give to violence when it appears in moral or spiritual contexts. A tenant's sliced-off ear, which is an object of at least momentary pleasure to Yeats, a kick given by an employer to his employee, which wins the approval of Lawrence—these are all too accurately representative of the nature of the political fantasies that Yeats and Lawrence built upon the perception of the loss of freedom and privilege, the loss of the sense of being. Yet we know that this violence stands against an extreme fate of which we are all conscious. We really know in our time what the death of the word can be—for that knowledge we have only to read an account of contemporary Russian literature. We really know what the death of the spirit means—we have seen it overtake whole peoples. Nor do we need to go beyond our own daily lives to become aware, if we dare to, of how we have conspired, in our very virtues, to bring about the devaluation of whatever is bold and assertive and free, replacing it by the bland, the covert, the manipulative. If we wish to understand the violence, the impulse toward charismatic power, of so much of our literature, we have but to consider that we must endure not only the threat to being which comes from without but also the seduction to non-being which establishes itself within. We need, in Coleridge's words, something to "startle this dull pain, and make it move and live." Violence is a means of self-definition; the bad conscience, Nietzsche says, assures us of our existence.

Wordsworth, then, is not separated from us by his preoccupation with being, for it is our preoccupation. Yet he is separated from us. His conception of being seems different from ours.

In Book Five of *The Prelude* Wordsworth gives us a satiric picture of the boy educated according to the "progressive" ideas of his day, and on the whole we follow him readily enough in the objections he makes to these ideas—this can be said even though it often happens that readers, misled by their preconceptions of Wordsworth, take his sarcasm seriously and suppose that he is actually praising "this model of a child." And we follow him when he speaks of the presumptuousness of pedagogical theorists, denouncing them as, in effect, engineers of the spirit: he flatters at least one element of our ambivalence toward the psychological expert. We are responsive to his notion of what a boy should be: "not . . . too good," "not unresentful where self-justified." Possibly we are not in perfect agreement with him on all points—perhaps we will feel that he has dealt rather too harshly with the alert political and social conscious-ness of the progressive child, or that he goes too far in thinking that a child's imagination should be fed on fanciful books; per-haps, too, the qualities of the boys he really admires would not be precisely the qualities we would specify—"Fierce, moody, patient, venturous, modest, shy." But on the whole his discussion of pedagogics appeals to the enlightened muddled concern with "adjustment" and "aggression" which occupies the P.T.A. segment of our minds, and if we have our reservation about de-tails we can at least, as I say, follow Wordsworth through most of his argument. But I think we cease to follow him when, in the course of the argument, he rises to one of his great poetical moments. This is the passage "There was a Boy. . . ." It was perhaps rather finer when it stood alone as a poem in itself in *Lyrical Ballads,* but it is still very fine in its place in *The Prelude,* where it follows the description of the model child. The Boy is described as having had a trick of imitating the hooting of owls, and at night he would call across Windermere, trying to get the owls to answer; and often they did answer, but sometimes they did not, and then the silence would be strange and signifi-cant.

> . . . In that silence, while he hung
> Listening, a gentle shock of mild surprise
> Has carried far into his heart the voice
> Of mountain torrents; or the visible scene
> Would enter unawares into his mind,
> With all its solemn imagery, its rocks,
> Its woods, and that uncertain heaven, received
> Into the bosom of the steady lake.

We may be ready enough to acknowledge the "beauty" of the poem, but the chances are that we will be rather baffled by its intention. We perceive that the Boy is obviously intended to represent something very good and right, meant to be an example of very full being. But what baffles us, what makes us wonder what the poem has to do with education and the development of personality, is that the Boy exercises no will, or at least, when his playful will is frustrated, is at once content with the pleasures that follow upon the suspended will. And as likely as not we will be impelled to refer the poem to that "mysticism" which is supposed to be an element of Wordsworth's mind. Now Wordsworth's mind does have an element of mysticism—it is that "normal mysticism" which, according to a recent writer on the Rabbis, marked the Rabbinical mind.[6] Wordsworth's mysticism, if we wish to call it that, consists of two elements, his conception of the world as being semantic, and his capacity for intense pleasure. When we speak of him as a mystic in any other sense, we are pretty sure to be expressing our incomprehension of the intensity with which he experienced his own being, and our incomprehension of the relation which his sentiment of being bore to his will. Thus, we have no trouble understanding him when, in Book Six of *The Prelude,* in the

---

[6] Max Kadushin, *The Rabbinical Mind* (New York: 1951). This impressive work of scholarship has received far less general notice than it deserves. I read it after I had written this essay—read it not only with admiration for its intellectual achievement but also with a peculiar personal pleasure, because its author, in his seminary days, had been one of the long-suffering men who tried to teach me Hebrew, with what success I have indicated; yet he did teach me—it was no small thing for a boy of twelve to be in relation with a serious scholar. Dr. Kadushin has been kind enough to tell me that what I have said about the Rabbis is not wrong. In revising my essay I have not tried to amend my primitive account by what is to be learned from Dr. Kadushin's presentation of the Rabbis in all their great complexity of thought. But the phrase, "normal mysticism," seemed too apt not to quote.

remarkable episode of the crossing of the Alps, he speaks of the
glory of the will.

> . . . Whether we be young or old,
> Our destiny, our being's heart and home,
> Is with infinitude, and only there;
> With hope it is, hope that can never die,
> Effort, and expectation, and desire,
> And something evermore about to be.

The note on which the will is affirmed is high, Miltonic—it
echoes the accents of Satan's speech in the Council of Hell; and
the passage resumes its movement with a line the martial tenor
of which we happily respond to: "Under such banners militant,
the soul . . ." But we are checked by what ensues:

> Under such banners militant, the soul
> Seeks for no trophies, struggles for no spoils
> That may attest her prowess, blest in thoughts
> That are their own perfection and reward,
> Strong in herself and in beatitude. . . .

The soul's energy is directed to the delight of the soul in itself.

Wordsworth is describing the action of what, at a later time,
a man of very different mind, Hegel, was to call a new human
faculty, the faculty of *Gemüt*. The word, I gather, is not entirely
susceptible of translation—"heart," with the implication of responsiveness, and of high-heartedness and large-heartedness, is
an approximation. Hegel defines his faculty of *Gemüt* as expressing itself as a desire, a will, which has "no particular aims, such
as riches, honors, and the like; in fact, it does not concern itself
with any worldly condition of wealth, prestige, etc., but with the
entire condition of the soul—a general sense of enjoyment."

Much that I have said about the tendency of our culture would
seem to deny the truth of Hegel's statement that *Gemüt* is one

of the characteristics of our time, and much more evidence might be adduced to confirm the impression that nothing could be less characteristic of our time than the faculty of *Gemüt,* that we scarcely conceive of it, let alone exercise it. Yet at the same time I think it is true to say that it plays in our culture a covert but very important part.

Of our negative response to *Gemüt,* to the "sentiment of Being," Mr. Eliot provides an instance—again, for it is Mr. Eliot's high gift to be as pertinent when we think him wrong as when we think him right. In *The Cocktail Party* there is a description of the two virtuous ways of life, that of "the common routine" and that of the spiritual heroism of the saint and martyr. The two ways, Mr. Eliot tells us, are of equal value; the way of the saint is not better than that of the householder. Yet when it comes to describing the life of the common routine, Mr. Eliot says of those who elect it that they

> Learn to avoid excessive expectation,
> Become tolerant of themselves and others,
> Giving and taking in the usual actions
> What there is to give and take. They do not repine;
> And are contented with the morning that separates
> And with the evening that brings together
> For casual talk before the fire
> Two people who know that they do not understand each other,
> Breeding children whom they do not understand
> And who will never understand them.

Well, few of us will want to say much for the life of the common routine, and no doubt, under the aspect of modern life with its terrible fatigues, and in the consciousness of its gross threats, the sort of thing that Mr. Eliot says here will be pretty nearly all that any of us will want to say. Yet if we think of the description of the common routine as being not merely the ex-

pression of one possible mood among many—and it is not merely
that: it is what it says it is, the description of a "way"—we must
find it very strange. There is in it no reference to the pain which
is an essential and not an accidental part of the life of the common routine. There is no reference to the principles, the ethical
discipline, by which the ordinary life is governed—all is habit.
There is no reference to the possibility of either joy or glory
—I use the Wordsworthian words by intention. The possibility
of *Gemüt* does not appear. Mr. Eliot does not say that his
couples are in Limbo, that they are in a condition of not-being,
which would of course be a true thing to say of many house-
holding couples: he is describing the virtuous way of life that
is alternative to the way of the saint. This failure to conceive
the actuality of the life of common routine is typical of modern
literature since, say, Tolstoi. I do not say this in order to suggest that domestic life, the common routine, in itself makes an
especially appropriate subject for literature—I don't think it
does—but in order to suggest a limitation of our conception of
the spiritual life. Mr. Eliot's representation of the two "ways"
exemplifies how we are drawn to the violence of extremity.
We imagine, with nothing in between, the dull not-being of
life, the intense not-being of death; but we do not imagine
being—we do not imagine that it can be a joy. We are in love,
at least in our literature, with the fantasy of death. Death and
suffering, when we read, are our only means of conceiving the
actuality of life.

Perhaps this is not new and we but intensify what is indige-
nous in our culture. Perhaps this is in the nature of life as Western culture has long been fated to see it. Perhaps it is inescapable
for us that the word "tragic" should be used as an ultimate
recommendation of a sense of life. Yet we, when we use the
word, do not really mean it in its old, complex, mysterious sense

—we mean something like "violent" or "conclusive": we mean death. And just here lies a paradox and our point. For it is precisely what Wordsworth implies by his passionate insistence on being, even at a very low level of consciousness, pride, and assertiveness, as well as at the highest level of quasi-mystic intensity, that validates a conception of tragedy, and a conception of heroism. The saintly martyrdom which Mr. Eliot represents in his play is of course not intended to be taken as tragic: the idea of martyrdom precludes the idea of tragedy. But if we ask why the martyrdom seems as factitious as it does, must we not answer that this is because it is presented in a system of feeling which sets very little store by—which, indeed, denies the possibility of—the "beatitude" which Wordsworth thought was the birthright of every human soul? And this seems to be borne out by the emphasis which Mr. Eliot puts on the peculiar horror of the mode of the martyr's death, as if only by an extremity of pain could we be made to realize that a *being* was actually involved, that a life has been sacrificed—or, indeed, has been lived.

Wordsworth's incapacity for tragedy has often been remarked on, and accurately enough. Yet we cannot conclude that Wordsworth's relation to tragedy is wholly negative. The possibility of tragic art depends primarily upon the worth we ascribe not to dying but to living, and to living in "the common routine." The power of the Homeric tragedy, for example, derives from the pathos, which the poet is at pains to bring before us repeatedly, of young men dying, of not seeing ever again the trees of their native farmsteads, of their parents never again admiring and indulging them, of the cessation of their being in the common routine. The tragic hero, Achilles, becomes a tragic hero exactly because he has made choice to give up the life of the common routine, which all his comrades desire, in favor of a briefer but more intense quality of being of transcendent glory.

The pathos of his particular situation becomes the great thing it is because of the respondent pathos of Hector and Priam, which is the pathos of the family and the common routine, which we understand less and less and find ourselves more and more uncomfortable with. And I think it can be shown that every tragic literature owes its power to the high esteem in which it holds the common routine, and the sentiment of being which arises from it, the elemental *given* of biology. And that is what Wordsworth had in mind when, in the "Preface" of 1800, defending the idea that poetry should give "immediate pleasure," he said that this idea was "a homage paid to the native and naked dignity of man, to the grand elementary principle of pleasure, by which he knows, and feels, and lives, and moves."

Yet if we are aware of the tendency of our literature I have exemplified by the passage from Mr. Eliot's play, we must at the same time be aware of the equally strong counter-tendency. In speaking of our alienation from Wordsworth, it has not been my intention to make a separation between Wordsworth and the literature of our time. The separation cannot be made. Wordsworth and the great writers of our time stand, as I have said, on the common ground of the concern with being and its problems —Wordsworth, indeed, may be said to have discovered and first explored the ground upon which our literature has established itself. Our hyperaesthesia, our preference for the apocalyptic subject and the charismatic style, do indeed constitute a taste which alienates many readers from Wordsworth, and no doubt the more if we believe, as some do, that it is a taste wholly appropriate to the actualities of our historical situation. Yet we can without too much difficulty become aware of how much of the Wordsworthian "mildness," which so readily irritates us, and how much of the Wordsworthian quietism (as I have called it), which dismays us, are in the grain of our literature, expressed through the very intensities which seem to deny them. Thus, to bring Wordsworth and James Joyce into conjunction might at first seem a joke or a paradox, or an excess of historicism, at best a mere device of criticism. We will at once be conscious of the calculated hauteur of Joyce's implied personality, the elaborations of his irony, the uncompromising challenge of his style and his manner, and by the association of contrast we will remember that horrendous moment in *The Prelude* when Wordsworth says, "My drift I fear/Is scarcely obvious." How can we fail to think only of the abysses of personality, theory, and culture that separate the two men? And yet when we have become acclimated to Joyce, when the charismatic legend becomes with familiarity not so fierce and the vatic paraphernalia of the style and method less intimidating, do we not find that we are involved in a conception of life that reiterates, in however different a tonality, the Wordsworthian vision? One of the striking things about *Ulysses* (to speak only of that work) is that the idea of evil plays so small a part in it. One hears a good deal about the essential Christian orthodoxy of Joyce, and perhaps this is an accurate opinion, but his orthodoxy, if he has it, takes no account of the evil which is so commonly affirmed by the literary expressions of orthodoxy; the conception of sin has but a tangential relevance to the book. The element of sexuality which plays so large a part in the story does not raise considerations of sin and evil; it is dealt with in the way of poetic naturalism. The character of Leopold Bloom, who figures in the life of Joyce's Poet much as the old men in Wordsworth figure in his life—met by chance and giving help of some transcendent yet essentially human kind—is conceived in Wordsworthian terms: in terms, that is, of his humbleness of spirit. If we speak of Wordsworth in reference to the Rabbis and their non-militancy, their indifference to the idea of evil, their acceptance of cosmic contradiction, are we not to say that Bloom is a Rabbinical character? It is exactly his non-militancy that makes him the object of general contempt and, on one occasion, of rage. It is just this that has captivated his author, as the contrast with the armed pride, the jealousy and desire for prestige, the bitter militancy of Stephen Dedalus. Leopold Bloom is deprived of every shred of dignity except the dignity of that innocence which for Joyce, as for Wordsworth, goes with the "sentiment of Being."

Again and again in our literature, at its most apocalyptic and intense, we find the impulse to create figures who are intended to suggest that life is justified in its elemental biological simplicity, and, in the manner of Wordsworth, these figures are conceived of as being of humble status and humble heart: Lawrence's simpler people or primitive people whose pride is only that of plants or animals; Dreiser's Jennie Gerhardt and Mrs. Griffiths, who stand as oases in the wide waste of their creator's dull representation of energy; Hemingway's waiters with their curious silent dignity; Faulkner's Negroes, of whom it is said, as so often it is said in effect of Wordsworth's people, *they endured;* and Faulkner's idiot boys, of whom it is to be said, *they are*—the list could be extended to suggest how great is the affinity of our literature with Wordsworth. And these figures express an intention which is to be discerned through all our literature —the intention to imagine, and to reach, a condition of the soul in which the will is freed from "particular aims," in which it is "strong in itself and in beatitude." At least as early as Balzac our literature has shown the will seeking its own negation—or, rather, seeking its own affirmation by its rejection of the aims which the world sets before it and by turning its energies upon itself in self-realization. Of this particular affirmation of the will Wordsworth is the proponent and the poet.

# George Orwell
# and the Politics of Truth

G EORGE ORWELL'S *Homage to Catalonia* is one of the important documents of our time. It is a very modest book—it seems to say the least that can be said on a subject of great magnitude. But in saying the least it says the most. Its manifest subject is a period of the Spanish Civil War, in which, for some months, until he was almost mortally wounded, its author fought as a soldier in the trenches. Everyone knows that the Spanish war was a decisive event of our epoch, everyone said so when it was being fought, and everyone was right. But the Spanish war lies a decade and a half behind us, and nowadays our sense of history is being destroyed by the nature of our history—our memory is short and it grows shorter under the rapidity of the assault of events. What once occupied all our minds and filled the musty meeting halls with the awareness of heroism and destiny has now become chiefly a matter for the historical scholar. George Orwell's book would make only a limited claim upon our attention if it were nothing more than a record of personal experiences in the Spanish war. But it is much more than this. It is a testimony to the nature of modern political life. It is also a demonstration on the part of its author of one of the right ways of confronting that life. Its importance is therefore of the present moment and for years to come.

A politics which is presumed to be available to everyone is a relatively new thing in the world. We do not yet know very much about it. Nor have most of us been especially eager to learn. In a politics presumed to be available to everyone, ideas and ideals play a great part. And those of us who set store by ideas and ideals have never been quite able to learn that, just because they do have power nowadays, there is a direct connection between their power and another kind of power, the old, unabashed, cynical power of force. We are always being surprised by this. The extent to which Communism made use of unregenerate force was perfectly clear years ago, but many of us found it impossible to acknowledge this fact because Communism spoke boldly to our love of ideas and ideals. We tried as hard as we could to believe that politics might be an idyl, only to discover that what we took to be a political pastoral was really a grim military campaign or a murderous betrayal of political allies, or that what we insisted on calling agrarianism was in actuality a new imperialism. And in the personal life what was undertaken by many good people as a moral commitment of the most disinterested kind turned out to be an engagement to an ultimate immorality. The evidence of this is to be found in a whole literary genre with which we have become familiar in the last decade, the personal confession of involvement and then of disillusionment with Communism.

Orwell's book, in one of its most significant aspects, is about disillusionment with Communism, but it is not a confession. I say this because it is one of the important positive things to say about *Homage to Catalonia,* but my saying it does not imply that I share the *a priori* antagonistic feelings of many people toward those books which, on the basis of experience, expose and denounce the Communist party. About such books people of liberal inclination often make uneasy and rather vindictive jokes. The jokes seem to me unfair and in bad taste. There is nothing shameful in the nature of these books. There is a good chance that the commitment to Communism was made in the first place for generous reasons, and it is certain that the revulsion was brought about by more than sufficient causes. And clearly there is nothing wrong in wishing to record the painful experience and to draw conclusions from it. Nevertheless, human nature being what it is—and in the uneasy readers of such books as well as in the unhappy writers of them—it is a fact that public confession does often appear in an unfortunate light, that its moral tone is less simple and true than we might wish it to be. But the moral tone of Orwell's book is uniquely simple and true. Orwell's ascertaining of certain political facts was not the occasion for a change of heart, or for a crisis of the soul. What he learned from his experiences in Spain of course pained him very much, and it led him to change his course of conduct. But it did not destroy him; it did not, as people say, cut the ground from under him. It did not shatter his faith in what he had previously believed, nor weaken his political impulse, nor even change its direction. It produced not a moment of guilt or self-recrimination.

Perhaps this should not seem so very remarkable. Yet who can doubt that it constitutes in our time a genuine moral triumph? It suggests that Orwell was an unusual kind of man, that he had a temper of mind and heart which is now rare, although we still respond to it when we see it.

It happened by a curious chance that on the day I agreed to write this essay as the introduction to the new edition of *Homage to Catalonia*, and indeed at the very moment that I was reaching for the telephone to tell the publisher that I would write it, a young man, a graduate student of mine, came in to see me, the purpose of his visit being to ask what I thought about his doing an essay on George Orwell. My answer, naturally, was ready, and when I had given it and we had been amused and pleased by the coincidence, he settled down for a chat about our common subject. But I asked him not to talk about Orwell. I didn't want to dissipate in talk what ideas I had, and also I didn't want my ideas crossed with his, which were sure to be very good. So for a while we merely exchanged bibliographical information, asking each other which of Orwell's books we had read and which we owned. But then, as if he could not resist making at least one remark about Orwell himself, he said suddenly in a very simple and matter-of-fact way, "He was a virtuous man." And we sat there, agreeing at length about this statement, finding pleasure in talking about it.

It was an odd statement for a young man to make nowadays, and I suppose that what we found so interesting about it was just this oddity—its point was in its being an old-fashioned thing to say. It was archaic in its bold commitment of sentiment, and it used an archaic word with an archaic simplicity. Our pleasure was not merely literary, not just a response to the remark's being so appropriate to Orwell, in whom there was indeed a quality of an earlier and simpler day. We were glad to be able to say it about anybody. One doesn't have the opportunity very often. Not that there are not many men who are good, but there are few men who, in addition to being good, have the simplicity and sturdiness and activity which allow us to say of them that they are virtuous men, for somehow to say that a man "is good," or even to speak of a man who "is virtuous," is not the same thing as saying, "He is a virtuous man." By some quirk of the spirit of the language, the form of that sentence brings out the primitive meaning of the word virtuous, which is not merely moral goodness, but also fortitude and strength in goodness.

Orwell, by reason of the quality that permits us to say of him that he was a virtuous man, is a figure in our lives. He was not a genius, and this is one of the remarkable things about him. His not being a genius is an element of the quality that makes him what I am calling a figure.

It has been some time since we in America have had literary figures—that is, men who live their visions as well as write them, who *are* what they write, whom we think of as standing for something as men because of what they have written in their books. They preside, as it were, over certain ideas and attitudes. Mark Twain was in this sense a figure for us, and so was William James. So too were Thoreau, and Whitman, and Henry Adams, and Henry James, although posthumously and rather uncertainly. But when in our more recent literature the writer is anything but anonymous, he is likely to be ambiguous and unsatisfactory as a figure, like Sherwood Anderson, or Mencken, or Wolfe, or Dreiser. There is something about the American character that does not take to the idea of the figure as the English character does. In this regard, the English are closer to the French than to us. Whatever the legend to the contrary, the English character is more strongly marked than ours, less reserved, less ironic, more open in its expression of willfulness and eccentricity and cantankerousness. Its manners are cruder and bolder. It is a demonstrative character—it shows itself, even shows off. Santayana, when he visited England, quite gave up the common notion that Dickens' characters are carica-tures. One can still meet an English snob so thunderingly shameless in his worship of the aristocracy, so explicit and de-monstrative in his adoration, that a careful, modest, ironic

American snob would be quite bewildered by him. And in modern English literature there have been many writers whose lives were demonstrations of the principles which shaped their writing. They lead us to be aware of the moral personalities that stand behind the work. The two Lawrences, different as they were, were alike in this: that they assumed the roles of their belief and acted them out on the stage of the world. In different ways this was true of Yeats, and of Shaw, and even of Wells. It is true of T. S. Eliot, for all that he has spoken against the claims of personality in literature. Even E. M. Forster, who makes so much of privacy, acts out in public the role of the private man, becoming for us the very spirit of the private life. He is not merely a writer, he is a figure.

Orwell takes his place with these men as a figure. In one degree or another they are geniuses, and he is not; if we ask what it is he stands for, what he is the the figure of, the answer is: the virtue of not being a genius, of fronting the world with nothing more than one's simple, direct, undeceived intelligence, and a respect for the powers one does have, and the work one undertakes to do. We admire geniuses, we love them, but they discourage us. They are great concentrations of intellect and emotion, we feel that they have soaked up all the available power, monopolizing it and leaving none for us. We feel that if we cannot be as they, we can be nothing. Beside them we are so plain, so hopelessly threadbare. How they glitter, and with what an imperious way they seem to deal with circumstances, even when they are wrong! Lacking their patents of nobility, we might as well quit. This is what democracy has done to us, alas—told us that genius is available to anyone, that the grace of ultimate prestige may be had by anyone, that we may all be princes and potentates, or saints and visionaries and holy martyrs, of the heart and mind. And then when it turns out that we are no such thing, it permits us to think that we aren't much of anything at all. In contrast with this cozening trick of democracy, how pleasant seems the old, reactionary Anglican phrase that used to drive people of democratic leanings quite wild with rage—"my station and its duties."

Orwell would very likely have loathed that phrase, but in a way he exemplifies its meaning. And it is a great relief, a fine sight, to see him doing this. His novels are good, quite good, some better than others, some of them surprising us by being so very much better than their modesty leads us to suppose they can be, all of them worth reading; but they are clearly not the work of a great or even of a "born" novelist. In my opinion, his satire on Stalinism, *Animal Farm,* was overrated —I think people were carried away by someone's reviving systematic satire for serious political purposes. His critical essays are almost always very fine, but sometimes they do not fully meet the demands of their subject—as, for example, the essay on Dickens. And even when they are at their best, they seem to have become what they are chiefly by reason of the very plainness of Orwell's mind, his simple ability to look at things in a downright, undeceived way. He seems to be serving not some dashing daimon but the plain, solid Gods of the Copybook Maxims. He is not a genius—what a relief! What an encouragement. For he communicates to us the sense that what he has done any one of us could do.

Or could do if we but made up our mind to do it, if we but surrendered a little of the cant that comforts us, if for a few weeks we paid no attention to the little group with which we habitually exchange opinions, if we took our chance of being wrong or inadequate, if we looked at things simply and directly, having in mind only our intention of finding out what they really are, not the prestige of our great intellectual act of looking at them. He liberates us. He tells us that we can understand our political and social life merely by looking around us; he frees us from the need for the inside dope. He implies that our job is not to be intellectual, certainly not to be intellectual in this fashion or that, but merely to be intelligent according to our lights—he restores the old sense of the democracy of the mind, releasing us from the belief that the mind can work only in a technical, professional way and that it must work competitively. He has the effect of making us believe that we may become full members of the society of thinking men. That is why he is a figure for us.

In speaking thus of Orwell, I do not mean to imply that his birth was presided over only by the Gods of the Copybook Maxims and not at all by the good fairies, or that he had no daimon. The good fairies gave him very fine free gifts indeed. And he had a strong daimon, but it was of an old-fashioned kind and it constrained him to the paradox—for such it is in our time—of taking seriously the Gods of the Copybook Maxims and putting his gifts at their service. Orwell responded to truths of more than one kind, to the bitter, erudite truths of the modern time as well as to the older and simpler truths. He would have quite understood what Karl Jaspers means when he recommends the "decision to renounce the absolute claims of the European humanistic spirit, to think of it as a stage of development rather than the living content of faith." But he was not interested in this development. What concerned him was survival, which he connected with the old simple ideas that are often not ideas at all but beliefs, preferences, and prejudices. In the modern world these had for him the charm and audacity of newly discovered truths. Involved as so many of us are, at least in our literary lives, in a bitter metaphysics of human nature, it shocks and dismays us when Orwell speaks in praise of such things as responsibility, and orderliness in the personal life, and fair play, and physical courage—even of snobbery and hypocrisy because they sometimes help to shore up the crumbling ramparts of the moral life.

It is hard to find personalities in the contemporary world who are analogous to Orwell. We have to look for men who have considerable intellectual power but who are not happy in the institutionalized life of intellectuality; who have a feeling for an older and simpler time, and a guiding awareness of the ordinary life of the people, yet without any touch of the sentimental malice of populism; and a strong feeling for the commonplace; and a direct, unabashed sense of the nation, even a conscious love of it. This brings Péguy to mind, and also Chesterton, and I think that Orwell does have an affinity with these men—he was probably unaware of it—which tells us something about him. But Péguy has been dead for quite forty years, and Chesterton (it is a pity) is at the moment rather dim for us, even for those of us who are Catholics. And of course Orwell's affinity with these men is limited by their Catholicism, for although Orwell admired some of the effects and attitudes of religion, he seems to have had no religious tendency in his nature, or none that went beyond what used to be called natural piety.

In some ways he seems more the contemporary of William Cobbett and William Hazlitt than of any man of our own century. Orwell's radicalism, like Cobbett's, refers to the past and to the soil. This is not uncommon nowadays in the social theory of literary men, but in Orwell's attitude there is none of the implied aspiration to aristocracy which so often marks literary agrarian ideas; his feeling for the land and the past simply served to give his radicalism a conservative—a conserving—cast, which is in itself attractive, and to protect his politics from the ravages of ideology. Like Cobbett, he does not dream of a new kind of man, he is content with the old kind, and what moves him is the desire that this old kind of man should have freedom, bacon, and proper work. He had the passion for the literal actuality of life as it is really lived which makes Cobbett's *Rural Rides* a classic, although a forgotten one; his own *The Road to Wigan Pier* and *Down and Out in Paris and London* are in its direct line. And it is not the least interesting detail in the similarity of the two men that both had a love affair with the English language. Cobbett, the self-educated agricultural laborer and sergeant major, was said by one of his enemies to handle the language better than anyone of his time, and he wrote a first-rate handbook of grammar and rhetoric; Orwell was obsessed by the deterioration of the English language in the hands of the journalists and pundits, and nothing in *Nineteen Eighty-Four* is more memorable than his creation of Newspeak.

Orwell's affinity with Hazlitt is, I suspect, of a more intimate temperamental kind, although I cannot go beyond the suspicion, for I know much less about Orwell as a person than about Hazlitt. But there is an unquestionable similarity in their intellectual temper which leads them to handle their political and literary opinions in much the same way. Hazlitt remained a Jacobin all his life, but his unshakable opinions never kept him from giving credit when it was deserved by a writer of the opposite persuasion, not merely out of chivalrous generosity but out of respect for the truth. He was the kind of passionate democrat who could question whether democracy could possibly produce great poetry, and his essays in praise of Scott and Coleridge, with whom he was in intense political disagreement, prepare us for Orwell on Yeats and Kipling.

The old-fashionedness of Orwell's temperament can be partly

explained by the nature of his relation to his class. This was by no means simple. He came from that part of the middle class whose sense of its status is disproportionate to its income, his father having been a subordinate officer in the Civil Service of India, where Orwell was born. (The family name was Blair, and Orwell was christened Eric Hugh; he changed his name, for rather complicated reasons, when he began to write.) As a scholarship boy he attended the expensive preparatory school of which Cyril Connolly has given an account in *Enemies of Promise*. Orwell appears there as a school "rebel" and "intellectual." He was later to write of the absolute misery of the poor boy at a snobbish school. He went to Eton on a scholarship, and from Eton to Burma, where he served in the police. He has spoken with singular honesty of the ambiguousness of his attitude in the imperialist situation. He disliked authority and the manner of its use, and he sympathized with the Burmese; yet at the same time he saw the need for authority and he used it, and he was often exasperated by the natives. When he returned to England on leave after five years of service, he could not bring himself to go back to Burma. It was at this time that, half voluntarily, he sank to the lower depths of poverty. This adventure in extreme privation was partly forced upon him, but partly it was undertaken to expiate the social guilt which he felt he had incurred in Burma. The experience seems to have done what was required of it. A year as a casual worker and vagrant had the effect of discharging Orwell's guilt, leaving him with an attitude toward the working class that was entirely affectionate and perfectly without sentimentality.

His experience of being declassed, and the effect which it had upon him, go far toward defining the intellectual quality of Orwell and the particular work he was to do. In the thirties the middle-class intellectuals made it a moral fashion to avow their guilt toward the lower classes and to repudiate their own class tradition. So far as this was nothing more than a moral fashion, it was a moral anomaly. And although no one can read history without being made aware of what were the grounds of this attitude, yet the personal claim to a historical guilt yields but an ambiguous principle of personal behavior, a still more ambiguous basis of thought. Orwell broke with much of what the English upper middle class was and admired. But his clear, uncanting mind saw that, although the morality of history might come to harsh conclusions about the middle class and although the practicality of history might say that its day was over, there yet remained the considerable residue of its genuine virtues. The love of personal privacy, of order, of manners, the ideal of fairness and responsibility—these are very simple virtues indeed and they scarcely constitute perfection of either the personal or the social life. Yet they still might serve to judge the present and to control the future.

Orwell could even admire the virtues of the lower middle class, which an intelligentsia always finds it easiest to despise. His remarkable novel, *Keep the Aspidistra Flying,* is a *summa* of all the criticisms of a commercial civilization that have ever been made, and it is a detailed demonstration of the bitter and virtually hopeless plight of the lower-middle-class man. Yet it insists that to live even in this plight is not without its stubborn joy. Péguy spoke of "fathers of families, those heroes of modern life"—Orwell's novel celebrates this biological-social heroism by leading its mediocre, middle-aging poet from the depths of splenetic negation to the acknowledgment of the happiness of fatherhood, thence to an awareness of the pleasures of marriage, and of an existence which, while it does not gratify his ideal conception of himself, is nevertheless his own. There is a dim, elegiac echo of Defoe and of the early days of the middle-class ascendancy as Orwell's sad young man learns to cherish the small personal gear of life, his own bed and chairs and saucepans—his own aspidistra, the ugly, stubborn, organic emblem of survival.

We may say that it was on his affirmation of the middle-class virtues that Orwell based his criticism of the liberal intelligentsia. The characteristic error of the middle-class intellectual of modern times is his tendency to abstractness and absoluteness, his reluctance to connect idea with fact, especially with personal fact. I cannot recall that Orwell ever related his criticism of the intelligentsia to the implications of *Keep the Aspidistra Flying,* but he might have done so, for the prototypical act of the modern intellectual is his abstracting himself from the life of the family. It is an act that has something about it of ritual thaumaturgy—at the beginning of our intellectual careers we are like nothing so much as those young members of Indian tribes who have had a vision or a dream which gives them power on condition that they withdraw from the ordinary life of the tribe. By intellectuality we are freed from the thralldom to the familial commonplace, from the materiality and concreteness by which it exists, the hardness of the cash and the hardness of getting it, the inelegance and intractability of family things. It gives us power over intangibles and imponderables, such as Beauty and Justice, and it permits us to escape the cosmic ridicule which in our youth we suppose is inevitably directed at those who take seriously the small concerns of the material quotidian world, which we know to be inadequate and doomed by the very fact that it is so absurdly *conditioned*—by things, habits, local and temporary customs, and the foolish errors and solemn absurdities of the men of the past.

The gist of Orwell's criticism of the liberal intelligentsia was that they refused to understand the conditioned nature of life. He never quite puts it in this way but this is what he means. He himself knew what war and revolution were really like, what government and administration were really like. From first-hand experience he knew what communism was. He could truly imagine what nazism was. At a time when most intellectuals still thought of politics as a nightmare abstraction, pointing to the fearfulness of the nightmare as evidence of their sense of reality, Orwell was using the imagination of a man whose hands and eyes and whole body were part of his thinking apparatus. Shaw had insisted upon remaining sublimely unaware of the Russian actuality; Wells had pooh-poohed the threat of Hitler and had written off as anachronisms the very forces that were at the moment shaping the world—racial pride, leader-worship, religious belief, patriotism, love of war. These men had trained the political intelligence of the intelligentsia, who now, in their love of abstractions, in their wish to repudiate the anachronisms of their own emotions, could not conceive of directing upon Russia anything like the same stringency of criticism they used upon their own nation. Orwell observed of them that their zeal for internationalism had led them to constitute Russia their new fatherland. And he had the simple courage to point out that the pacifists preached their doctrine under condition of the protection of the British navy, and that, against Germany and Russia, Gandhi's passive resistance would have been of no avail.

He never abated his anger against the established order. But a paradox of history had made the old British order one of the still beneficent things in the world, and it licensed the possibility of a social hope that was being frustrated and betrayed almost everywhere else. And so Orwell clung with a kind of wry, grim pride to the old ways of the last class that had ruled the old order. He must sometimes have wondered how it came about that he should be praising sportsmanship and gentleman-liness and dutifulness and physical courage. He seems to have thought, and very likely he was right, that they might come in handy as revolutionary virtues—he remarks of Rubashov, the central character of Arthur Koestler's novel *Darkness at Noon,* that he was firmer in loyalty to the revolution than certain of his comrades because he had, and they had not, a bourgeois past. Certainly the virtues he praised were those of survival, and they had fallen into disrepute in a disordered world.

Sometimes in his quarrel with the intelligentsia Orwell seems to sound like a leader-writer for the *Times* in a routine war-time attack on the highbrows.

... The general weakening of imperialism, and to some extent of the whole British morale, that took place during the nineteen thirties, was partly the work of the left-wing intelligentsia, itself a kind of growth that sprouted from the stagnation of the Empire.

The mentality of the English left-wing intelligentsia can be studied in half a dozen weekly and monthly papers. The immediately striking thing about all these papers is their generally negative querulous attitude, their complete lack at all times of any constructive suggestion. There is little in them except the irresponsible carping of people who have never been and never expect to be in a position of power.

During the past twenty years the negative faineant outlook which has been fashionable among the English left-wingers, the sniggering of the intellectuals at patriotism and physical cour-age, the persistent effort to chip away at English morale and spread a hedonistic, what-do-I-get-out-of-it attitude to life, has done nothing but harm.

But he was not a leader-writer for the *Times*. He had fought in Spain and nearly died there, and on Spanish affairs his position had been the truly revolutionary one. The passages I have quoted are from his pamphlet, *The Lion and the Unicorn,* a persuasive statement of the case for socialism in Britain.

Toward the end of his life Orwell discovered another reason for his admiration of the old middle-class virtues and his criticism of the intelligentsia. Walter Bagehot used to speak of the political advantages of *stupidity,* meaning by the word a concern for one's own private material interests as a political motive which was preferable to an intellectual, theoretical interest. Orwell, it may be said, came to respect the old bourgeois virtues because they were stupid—that is, because they resisted the power of abstract ideas. And he came to love things, material possessions, for the same reason. He did not in the least become what is called "anti-intellectual"—this was simply not within the range of possibility for him—but he began to fear that the commitment to abstract ideas could be far more maleficent than the commitment to the gross materiality of property had ever been. The very stupidity of things has something human about it, something meliorative, something even liberating. Together with the stupidity of the old unthinking virtues it stands against the ultimate and absolute power which the unconditioned idea can develop. The essential point of *Nineteen Eighty-Four* is just this, the danger of the ultimate and absolute power which mind can develop when it frees itself from conditions, from the bondage of things and history.

But this, as I say, is a late aspect of Orwell's criticism of intellectuality. Through the greater part of his literary career his criticism was simpler and less extreme. It was as simple as this: that the contemporary intellectual class did not think and did not really love the truth.

In 1937 Orwell went to Spain to observe the civil war and to write about it. He stayed to take part in it, joining the militia as a private. At that time each of the parties still had its own militia units, although these were in process of being absorbed into the People's Army. Because his letters of introduction were from people of a certain political group in England, the ILP,[1] which had connections with the POUM,[2] Orwell joined a unit of that party in Barcelona. He was not at the time sympathetic to the views of his comrades and their leaders. During the days of interparty strife, the POUM was represented in Spain and abroad as being a Trotskyist party. In point of fact it was not, although it did join with the small Trotskyist party to oppose certain of the policies of the dominant Communist party. Orwell's own preference, at the time of his enlistment, was for the Communist party line, and because of this he looked forward to an eventual transfer to a Communist unit.

It was natural, I think, for Orwell to have been a partisan of the Communist program for the war. It recommended itself to most people on inspection by its apparent simple common sense. It proposed to fight the war without any reference to any particular political idea beyond a defense of democracy from a fascist enemy. When the war was won, the political and social problems would be solved, but until the war should be won, any debate over these problems was to be avoided as leading only to the weakening of the united front against Franco.

Eventually Orwell came to understand that this was not the practical policy he had at first thought it to be. His reasons need not be reiterated here—he gives them with characteristic cogency and modesty in the course of his book, and under the gloomy but probably correct awareness that, the economic and

[1] Independent Labour Party.
[2] *Partido Obrero de Unificación Marxista*—Party of Marxist Unification.

social condition of Spain being what it was, even the best policies must issue in some form of dictatorship In sum, he believed that the war was revolutionary or nothing, and that the people of Spain would not fight and die for a democracy which was admittedly to be a bourgeois democracy.

But Orwell's disaffection from the Communist party was not the result of a difference of opinion over whether the revolution should be instituted during the war or after it. It was the result of his discovery that the Communist party's real intention was to prevent the revolution from ever being instituted at all —"The thing for which the Communists were working was not to postpone the Spanish revolution till a more suitable time, but to make sure it never happened." The movement of events, led by the Communists, who had the prestige and the supplies of Russia, was always to the right, and all protest was quieted by the threat that the war would be lost if the ranks were broken, which in effect meant that Russian supplies would be withheld if the Communist lead was not followed. Meanwhile the war was being lost because the government more and more distrusted the non-Communist militia units, particularly those of the Anarchists. "I have described," Orwell writes, "how we were armed, or not armed, on the Aragon front. There is very little doubt that arms were deliberately withheld lest too many of them should get into the hands of the Anarchists, who would afterwards use them for a revolutionary purpose; consequently, the big Aragon offensive which would have made Franco draw back from Bilbao and possibly from Madrid, never happened."

At the end of April, after three months on the Aragon front, Orwell was sent to Barcelona on furlough. He observed the change in morale that had taken place since the days of his enlistment—Barcelona was no longer the revolutionary city it had been. The heroic days were over. The militia, which had done such splendid service at the beginning of the war, was now being denigrated in favor of the People's Army, and its members were being snubbed as seeming rather queer in their revolutionary ardor, not to say dangerous. The tone of the black market and of privilege had replaced the old idealistic puritanism of even three months earlier. Orwell observed this but drew no conclusions from it. He wanted to go to the front at Madrid, and in order to do so he would have to be transferred to the International Column, which was under the control of the Communists. He had no objection to serving in a Communist command and, indeed, had resolved to make the transfer. But he was tired and in poor health and he waited to conclude the matter until another week of his leave should be up. While he delayed, the fighting broke out in Barcelona.

In New York and in London the intelligentsia had no slightest doubt of what had happened—could not, indeed, have conceived that anything might have happened other than what they had been led to believe had actually happened. The Anarchists, together with the "Trotskyist" POUM—so it was said —had been secreting great stores of arms with a view to an uprising that would force upon the government their premature desire for collectivization. And on the third of May their plans were realized when they came out into the streets and captured the Telephone Exchange, thus breaking the united front in an extreme manner and endangering the progress of the war. But Orwell in Barcelona saw nothing like this. He was under the orders of the POUM, but he was not committed to its line, and certainly not to the Anarchist line, and he was sufficiently sympathetic to the Communists to wish to join one of their units. What he saw he saw as objectively as a man might ever see anything. And what he records is now, I believe, accepted as the essential truth by everyone whose judgment is worth regarding. There were no great stores of arms cached by the Anarchists and the POUM—there was an actual shortage of arms in their ranks. But the Communist-controlled government had been building up the strength of the Civil Guard, a gendarmerie which was called "nonpolitical" and from which workers were excluded. That there had indeed been mounting tension between the government and the dissident forces is beyond question, but the actual fighting was touched off by acts of provocation committed by the government itself—shows of military strength, the call to all private persons to give up arms, attacks on Anarchist centers, and, as a climax, the attempt to take over the Telephone Exchange, which since the beginning of the war had been run by the Anarchists.

It would have been very difficult to learn anything of this in New York or London. The periodicals that guided the thought of left-liberal intellectuals knew nothing of it, and had no wish to learn. As for the aftermath of the unhappy uprising, they appeared to have no knowledge of that at all. When Barcelona was again quiet—some six thousand Assault Guards were imported to quell the disturbance—Orwell returned to his old front. There he was severely wounded, shot through the neck; the bullet just missed the windpipe. After his grim hospitalization, of which he writes so lightly, he was invalided to Barcelona. He returned to find the city in process of being purged. The POUM and the Anarchists had been suppressed; the power of the workers had been broken and the police hunt was on. The jails were already full and daily becoming fuller —the most devoted fighters for Spanish freedom, men who had given up everything for the cause, were being imprisoned under the most dreadful conditions, often held incommunicado, often never to be heard of again. Orwell himself was suspect and in danger because he had belonged to a POUM regiment, and he stayed in hiding until, with the help of the British consul, he was able to escape to France. But if one searches the liberal periodicals, which have made the cause of civil liberties their own, one can find no mention of this terror. Those members of the intellectual class who prided themselves upon their political commitment were committed not to the fact but to the abstraction.[3]

And to the abstraction they remained committed for a long time to come. Many are still committed to it, or nostalgically wish they could be. If only life were not so tangible, so concrete, so made up of facts that are at variance with each other; if only the things that people say are good things were really good; if only the things that are pretty good were entirely good and we were not put to the everlasting necessity of qualifying and discriminating; if only politics were not a matter of power—*then* we should be happy to put our minds to politics, *then* we should consent to think!

But Orwell had never believed that the political life could be an intellectual idyl. He immediately put his mind to the politics he had experienced. He told the truth, and told it in an exemplary way, quietly, simply, with due warning to the reader that it was only one man's truth. He used no political

[3] In looking through the files of *The Nation* and the *New Republic* for the period of the Barcelona fighting, I have come upon only one serious contradiction of the interpretation of events that constituted the editorial position of both periodicals. This was a long letter contributed by Bertram Wolfe to the correspondence columns of *The Nation*. When this essay first appeared, some of my friends took me to task for seeming to imply that there were no liberal or radical intellectuals who did not accept the interpretations of *The Nation* and the *New Republic*. There were indeed such liberal or radical intellectuals. But they were relatively few in number and they were treated with great suspiciousness and even hostility by the liberal and radical intellectuals as a class. It is as a class that Orwell speaks of the intellectuals of the left in the thirties, and I follow him in this.

jargon, and he made no recriminations. He made no effort to show that his heart was in the right place, or the left place. He was not interested in where his heart might be thought to be, since he knew where it was. He was interested only in telling the truth. Not very much attention was paid to his truth—*Homage to Catalonia* sold poorly in England, it had to be remaindered, it was not published in America, and the people to whom it should have said most responded to it not at all.

Its particular truth refers to events now far in the past, as in these days we reckon our past. It does not matter the less for that—this particular truth implies a general truth which, as now we cannot fail to understand, must matter for a long time to come. And what matters most of all is our sense of the man who tells the truth.

# Flaubert's Last Testament

## [ 1 ]

FLAUBERT died suddenly in 1880, having brought close to its end but leaving unfinished and unrevised the novel that had occupied his thought for eight years. The entire dedication of himself with which Flaubert responded to the claims of art is of course the very essence of his legend, but to *Bouvard and Pécuchet* he gave a special and savage devotion which went beyond the call of literary duty as even he understood it. The book was to him more than a work of art; it was a deed. At the moment of what he conceived to be the ultimate defeat of true culture, it was an act of defiance and revenge. Flaubert was not unique in nineteenth-century France for his belief that bourgeois democracy was bringing about the death of mind, beauty, literature, and greatness; this opinion, among the distinguished writers of the century, was virtually a commonplace. But he was unique in the immediacy and simplicity with which he experienced the debacle—"I can no longer talk with anyone without growing angry; and whenever I read anything by one of my contemporaries I rage." [1] He was unique too in the

[1] The quotations from Flaubert's letters are from the admirable *Selected Letters of Gustave Flaubert* edited and translated by Francis Steegmuller. The quotations from *Bouvard and Pécuchet* are from the version of E. W. Stonier and T. W. Earp.

necessity he felt to see the crisis in all its possible specificity of detail. For him the modern barbarism was not merely a large general tendency which could be comprehended by a large general emotion; he was constrained to watch it with a compulsive and obsessive awareness of its painful particularities. He was made rabid, to use his own word, by *this* book, *this* phrase, *this* solecism, *this* grossness of shape or form, *this* debasement of manners, *this* hollow imitation of thought. He was beyond believing that he could do anything to stem or divert the flood of swinishness, as he called it, that was sweeping away every hope of the good life—*Bouvard and Pécuchet* is a triumph of the critical mind, but if we suppose criticism to be characterized by the intention to correct and reform, the book cannot be called a work of criticism. In its intention it is to be compared not with any other literary work but with the stand of Roland at Roncesvalles. No less beset than the hero, no less hopeless, no less grim, and no less grimly glad, Flaubert resolves that while the breath of life is in him he will give blow for blow and pile up the corpses of his enemies as a monument to the virtues they despise and he adores.

His long fierce passion for the book was not matched by the expectation of certain of his friends who were most competent to estimate the chances of its success. "I am preparing a book," he wrote to Turgenev in November of 1872, "in which I shall spit out my bile." But Turgenev grew troubled, and so did Taine and Zola, because Flaubert was precisely not spitting out his bile. The new novel, as Flaubert said of it, was to be "a kind of encyclopedia made into farce," and he devoured libraries, his notebooks grew ever more numerous, and his pride in them grew with their number; he was to brag that he had read fifteen hundred books in preparation for the novel. Anyone who loved Flaubert must have been dismayed as he gave year after year of his life to gathering the materials for a massive joke which was no doubt very funny but surely not so funny as to need this sacrificial attention from a man of genius. His love of research, his insatiable craving for particularity, was said to have spoiled *Salammbô* by overloading it with antiquarian lumber. Now it threatened to defeat the new work. Turgenev and Taine believed that an intellectual satire such as Flaubert planned must be short if it was to be read; Turgenev pointed to Swift and Voltaire in support of his opinion that *Bouvard and Pécuchet* must be treated *presto*. But Flaubert persisted in his extravagance. What he wanted to do, he said, was nothing less than to take account of the whole intellectual life of France. "If it were treated briefly, made concise and light, it would be a fantasy—more or less witty, but without weight or plausibility; whereas if I give it detail and development I will seem to be believing my own story, and it can be made into something serious and even frightening." And he believed that it was exactly by an excess of evidence that he would avoid pedantry.

The misgivings of his friends seemed in part justified by the public response to the book when it was published in the year after Flaubert's death. At first it was accepted merely as a "document," that is, its interest seemed to derive less from itself than from its connection with its author. But as the years passed, the first impression was corrected. With due allowance made for its unfinished, unrevised state, but quite in its own right, *Bouvard and Pécuchet* was given its place beside the great works of Flaubert's canon. Its pleasures are granted to be very different from those of *Madame Bovary* and *A Sentimental Education,* but French readers find in it a peculiar interest and charm consonant with its nature.

Its nature is singular. We cannot go so far as to say with

Ezra Pound that the novel "can be regarded as the inaugura-
tion of a new form which has no precedents," and in any case,
Mr. Pound, after having said that "neither *Gargantua,* nor *Don
Quixote,* nor Sterne's *Tristram Shandy* had furnished the ar-
chetype," goes on to show its clear connection with at least
the first-named book. And if it can be argued that *Bouvard and
Pécuchet,* in its character of "a kind of encyclopedia made into
farce," has no specific literary genre except perhaps that which
is comprised by *Gargantua,* it is still true that there are a sufficient number of works sufficiently analogous with it in one
respect or another to constitute, if not a genre, then at least a
tradition in which it may be placed. Yet its singularity must
not be slighted.

If we try to say what was the characteristic accomplishment
of the French novelists of the nineteenth century, we can scarcely
help concluding that it was the full, explicit realization of the
idea of society as a definitive external circumstance, the main
*condition,* of the individual life. American literature of the
great age was, as D. H. Lawrence was the first to see, more
profound in this respect than the French, in that it went deeper
into the unconscious life of society; and in England, Dickens
in his way and the later Trollope in his were more truly perceptive of social motives and movements. But the French
achievement was more explicit than either the American or
the English; it made itself available to more people. Almost,
we might be moved to say, it made itself too available: it is the
rare person who can receive the full news of the inherent social
immorality without injury to his own morality, without injury,
indeed, to his own intellect—nothing can be so stultifying as
the simple, unelaborated belief that society is a fraud. Yet with
the explicit social intelligence of the great French novels we
dare not quarrel—it is a *given* of our culture, it is one of the

ineluctable elements of our modern fate, and on the whole one of the nobler elements. What *Bouvard and Pécuchet* adds to this general fund of social intelligence is the awareness of the part that is played in our modern life by ideas—not merely by assumptions, which of course have always played their part in every society, but by ideas as they are formulated and developed in books. The originality of Flaubert's perception lies in its intensity; other novelists before Flaubert had been aware of the importance of ideas in shaping the lives of their heroes, and Flaubert himself, in *A Sentimental Education,* had shown Frédéric Moreau living in a kind of ideological zoo—Sénécal, Regimbart, Deslauriers, Pellerin, all have learned from books the roar or squeal or grunt by which they identify themselves. But in *Bouvard and Pécuchet* the books themselves are virtually the *dramatis personae;* it is they, even more than the actual people of the Norman village, that constitute reality for the two comic heroes. Through this extravagance Flaubert signalizes the ideological nature of modern life.

No one has followed Flaubert in his enterprise. In the essay to which I have referred, Mr. Pound was bringing, in 1922, the first news of Joyce's *Ulysses* to the readers of the *Mercure de France,* and he spoke at some length of the connection that is to be found between *Ulysses* and *Bouvard and Pécuchet.* "Between 1880 and the year *Ulysses* was begun," he says, "no one had the courage to make a gigantic collection of absurdities, nor the patience to seek out the man-type, the most general generalization"—and he goes on to speak of Leopold Bloom as being, like Bouvard and Pécuchet, "the basis of democracy, the man who believes what he reads in the papers." The connection between the two novels is certainly worth remarking, but although *Ulysses* does indeed resemble *Bouvard and Pécuchet* in its encyclopedic effect, the use made of the absurdities they

collect is very different in the one novel and in the other. The
difference is defined by the dissimilar intellectual lives of Leopold Bloom and Bouvard and Pécuchet. To Bloom, ideas are
the furniture or landscape of his mind, while to Bouvard and
Pécuchet they exist, as I have suggested, as characters in the
actual world. Bloom's ideas are notions; they are bits and pieces
of fact and approximations and adumbrations of thought pieced
together from newspapers and books carelessly read; Bloom
means to look them up and get them straight but he never
does. They are subordinate to his emotions, to which they lend
substance and color. If a judgment is passed upon them by
the author, it is of an oblique sort and has to do with their
tone, with their degree of vulgarity, not with their inner con-
sistency or cogency. But Bouvard and Pécuchet are committed
to ideas and confront them fully. They amass books and study
them. Ideas are life and death to them.

There is no necessity to choose between the two conceptions
of what Mr. Pound called "the man-type, the most general
generalization." Leopold Bloom represents much of the modern
mind from the lowest to the highest. His representativeness
probably needs less to be insisted on than that of Bouvard and
Pécuchet, who stand for the condition of life of any reader of
this book, of any person who must decide by means of some
sort of intellectual process what is the correct *theory* of raising
his children, or what is the right *principle* of education; or
whom he shall be psychoanalyzed by—a Freudian, a Reichian,
a Washingtonian; whether he "needs" religion, and if so, which
confession is most appropriate to his temperament and cultural
background; what kind of architecture he shall adopt for his
house, and what the true theory of the modern is; what kind
of heating is best suited to his life-style; how he shall feel about
the State; about the Church; about Labor; about China; about

Russia; about India. If we try to say how the world has changed from, say, two hundred years ago, we must see that it is in the respect that the conscious mind has been brought to bear upon almost every aspect of life; that ideas, good, bad, indifferent, are of the essence of our existence. That is why Flaubert was made "rabid" by his perception of stupidity. And if we look to see if anyone has matched Flaubert in the passion of his response to ideas, I think we find that Nietzsche alone saw the modern world as Flaubert did, and with Flaubert's intensity of passion.

But when we have become aware of the singularity of *Bouvard and Pécuchet,* we must be no less aware of the tradition in which its singularity exists. As for the novel's connection with Rabelais, this may be observed even in certain aspects of the prose, not necessarily as a result of influence, perhaps only because of the effect of an analogous subject matter. "He planted passion-flowers in the shade, pansies in the sun, covered hyacinths with manure, watered the lilies after they had flowered, destroyed the rhododendrons by cutting them back, stimulated the fuchsias with glue, and roasted the pomegranate tree by exposing it to the kitchen fire"—the errors of this catalogue are committed not by the infant Gargantua but by Pécuchet. Rabelais knew nothing of encyclopedias but he too wrote "a sort of encyclopedia made into farce." His intention was in part that of Flaubert—it was the intention of burlesque, the mockery of learning. But only in part: Rabelais had also the intention of which Flaubert's is the exact inversion. It is no doubt all too easy to reduce Rabelais to a classroom example of the high optimism of the early Renaissance, and to make more naïve than it really is his humanistic delight in the arts, sciences, crafts, and exercises which are available to man. Yet the optimism and the humanistic delight are certainly of the essence of Rabelais and they are specifically controverted in *Bouvard and Pécuchet*. We have but to look at the respective treatments of gymnastics to see how Flaubert stands Rabelais on his head—Gargantua's friend Gymnast can make any demand upon his agility and strength, to Rabelais' great delight, but nothing is sadder than the middle-aged Bouvard and Pécuchet putting themselves to school to the regimen and apparatus of Amoros's manual of physical culture, which, absurd as it is, descends in a direct line from the Renaissance idea of the Whole Man, the vaunting mind in the vaulting body.

If we speak of encyclopedias, there is one actual encyclopedia which we must have in recollection—the great *Encyclopédie* itself. Flaubert never makes Diderot the object of his satire— one may well suppose that the author of *Rameau's Nephew* was the last man in the world with whom Flaubert would have sought a quarrel—but Diderot's great enterprise of the *Encyclopédie,* which derived its impulse as much from the spirit of Rabelais as from the spirit of Bacon, is the heroic and optimistic enterprise of which the researches of *Bouvard and Pécuchet* are the comic and pessimistic counterpart. To have thought of Diderot busily running about France, taking notes on this trade or that process, learning how spinning or weaving or smelting or brewing was done, so that all the world might have a healthy knowledge of the practical arts, would be to have the inspiration for those scenes in which Bouvard and Pécuchet undertake to deal with practical life, to grow their own food and to preserve it, to make their own cordial ("Bouvarine," it is to be called!). *Bouvard and Pécuchet* in its despair that anything at all can be done is the negation of the morning confidence and hope of the *Encyclopédie*.

Which brings us to the third book of *Gulliver's Travels*.

The Voyage to Laputa, in which Swift satirizes the scientific theories of his day, may be thought of as the ambivalent prolegomenon to the *Encyclopédie*—ambivalent because Swift was Baconian in his conception of the practical aim of science but anti-Baconian in his contempt for any kind of scientific method he knew of, even Bacon's positivism. In the expression of his scorn he provides a striking precedent for *Bouvard and Pécuchet,* which had for its explanatory subtitle, "The failings of the methods of science." The analogy that may be drawn between Flaubert's book and Swift's goes considerably beyond what is suggested merely by the Voyage to Laputa—it leads us, indeed, to the personal similarity of Flaubert and Swift. But this may better be observed in another place.

Mr. Pound, having particularly in mind the encyclopedic nature of *Bouvard and Pécuchet,* finds *Don Quixote* to be a very different kind of thing—"Cervantes parodied but a single literary folly, the chivalric folly." Yet it is not the parody of the chivalric idea that in itself makes *Don Quixote* what it is, but rather the complex drama that results from putting an elaborate idea to the test in the world of actuality. Flaubert said of Madame Bovary that she was the sister of Don Quixote; Bouvard and Pécuchet are at least consanguineous enough to be cousins. And their idea, despite its encyclopedic mutations, is, after all, as much a unity as Don Quixote's: they believe that the world yields to mind. And if *Don Quixote,* then certainly *Candide,* which also tests an idea in the laboratory of the world. The conclusion of *Bouvard and Pécuchet,* "Let us return to copying," has not become proverbial only because its proverbial possibilities have been pre-empted by "Let us cultivate our garden."

Then the second act of *The Bourgeois Gentleman,* in which

Monsieur Jourdain receives instruction from the professors of
the sciences, arts, and graces, may be thought of as a small
encyclopedia in the form of a farce and as the model for this
history of the bourgeois savants. The *Dunciad* must not go
without mention. And the ingenious reader may amuse himself by discovering all the analogies that may be drawn between
*Bouvard and Pécuchet* and *Faust*.

[ 2 ]

"*Bouvard et Pécuchet sont-ils des imbeciles?*" The blunt
question is the title of an essay, notable in the history of Flaubert
criticism, which was published in 1914 by the eminent scholar
René Dumesnil. It is the question which lies at the heart of
the ambiguity of *Bouvard and Pécuchet*.

It will perhaps seem strange that ambiguity should be im-
puted to the novel. In England and America more people know
about *Bouvard and Pécuchet* than have read it. The author's
purpose as stated in his famous correspondence, and also the
outline of the story, are part of our general literary information. Neither the purpose nor the story suggests the possibility
of ambiguity. Flaubert's avowed intention, that of pillorying
the culture of bourgeois democracy, does not seem likely to
induce or even permit more than one meaning to appear. As
for his plan of having two simple copying clerks undertake to
master, seriatim, all the sciences and disciplines, and to come
to grief or boredom with each one, it seems clear and schematic
to a degree, even to a fault—it is hard to see why it should
not be entirely within the control of the author's equally clear
purpose. Yet it has been said by a French writer that of all the
works of Flaubert it is *Bouvard and Pécuchet* that gives the
critics the most trouble; that it is a book which is intricate,

complex, and difficult to analyze; that its meaning is hard to come at.[2]

Indeed, so great is the ambiguity of *Bouvard and Pécuchet* that it is possible to conclude that the book quite fails to be what Flaubert intended it to be. Which need not, of course, prevent it from being something else of a very good sort.

The trouble starts with the fact that Bouvard and Pécuchet, as Dumesnil demonstrated, are *not* imbeciles. Perhaps it is too much to say, as Dumesnil does say, that they have the souls of apostles, but imbeciles they certainly are not, and we shall be able to go considerably further in their praise than this mere negation. There can be no doubt that Flaubert began with the intention of making them as foolish and ridiculous as possible. We are surely not free to suppose that he had any inclination to show them mercy because they were poor clerks and lived very limited lives. When the word bourgeoisie came to be used in this country in a social-political sense, it was likely to be restricted in its reference to people of pretty solid establishment. For the social group more or less analogous to that to which Bouvard and Pécuchet belonged we used other words, choosing them according to our political disposition—"white-collar workers," "office proletariat," "little people." But Flaubert made no such distinction. For him the bourgeoisie was the bourgeoisie from top to bottom. He saw the characteristics and the power of the class as continuous from the wealthy to the poor. If he had thought to call the small bourgeoisie the "little people," he would have done so contemptuously, having reference to the size of their ideas and ideals and impulses. And he feared them exactly for this littleness, which he believed they wanted to impose upon the world. It was by no means the straitened lives that Bouvard and Pécuchet lived for forty-seven years until the

[2] Claude Digeon, in his *Le Dernier Visage de Flaubert* (Paris: 1946), p. 94.

great moment when they met each other that induced Flaubert to let them off from being imbeciles. No doubt in reference to just this hole-and-corner existence he had at one time cruelly planned to call the book "The History of Two Cockroaches."

But two cockroaches cannot be friends with each other. And François Denys Bartholomée Bouvard and Juste Romain Cyrille Pécuchet—their Christian names once mentioned in their history are forever forgotten and may as well be memorialized here —are truly friends. This fact is of decisive importance in the novel—it defeats whatever intention Flaubert may have had to make his protagonists contemptible. To Flaubert friendship was not merely a relation: it was a virtue, as it was for Montaigne, as it was for Swift.

Bouvard and Pécuchet are able to be friends because they are sufficiently different in their natures, although at one in their minds. Bouvard, as the sound of his name suggests, is the fleshier of the two, the more rotund, and the easier-going, the more sentimental, sensual, and worldly. Pécuchet, in accordance with his name, is lean and stringy; he is puritanical, passionate, pessimistic—a little more *sincere* than Bouvard. (Flaubert set great store by their names. When he overheard Zola say that he had found the perfect name for a character, Bouvard, he turned pale, and in the greatest agitation begged Zola not to use it. And he was much troubled when a banker named Pécuchet, a man he respected, played an important part in his financial life in 1875; the point of delicacy was settled by M. Pécuchet's death.)

Once in their life together, after many frustrations, at a moment when they are nervous and depressed, Bouvard and Pécuchet find that they can't stand the sight of each other; this is natural and transitory, and it but serves to emphasize the fullness and constancy of their devotion to each other. Their manner of life, we must recognize, has great charm. They are much harassed, much frustrated by practical as well as by intellectual matters, but their housekeeping, which is omnipresent in the story, is a pleasure to read about. Even when the economy falls quite to pieces and becomes sordid, it never quite belies the rich common poetry of their first meal, their first evening, their first morning in their own home. From their establishment we derive the pleasure which is afforded by the living arrangements of *Robinson Crusoe* or *The Swiss Family Robinson,* or Boffin's Bower, or Sherlock Holmes's rooms in Baker Street. Their enterprises are based on innocence and a pleasant sufficiency: they have a good deal in common with the respected author of "Speculations on the Source of the Hempstead Ponds, with some Observations of the Theory of Tittlebats," for Mr. Pickwick, another superannuated bourgeois bachelor, was devoted to the life of the mind, and his scientific adventures, although more primitive than those of Bouvard and Pécuchet, are alike in kind. They have affinity with Tom Sawyer—they are consciously boyish in their dreams of glory, in their dreams of love; for a moment, in their hydrotherapeutic phase, they have their Jackson's Island and are seen naked as Red Indians and gleefully splashing each other from their adjoining baths. Their life, despite its disappointments, is a kind of idyl, and it approaches the pastoral convention— there is no reason not to think of them as two shepherds tending their woolly flocks of ideas. Who would not want to read Bouvard's "Lament for Pécuchet," or, for the matter of that, Pécuchet's "Elegy for Bouvard," whichever came first; and whose heart would not be wrung by the event either poem recorded and the loneliness of the survivor at the double copying desk, the contriving of which had been the last ingenuity of the two friends?

Had they lived alone and pursued their studies and projects alone, it is possible that imbecility might have descended upon the mind of each. It is not until they meet each other that they really begin their intellectual life. Although they are always at one in their enthusiasm, they take sufficiently different views of questions to create between them a degree of dialectic; Flaubert, like Plato, conceived of friendship as one of the conditions of thought. Love and logic go together.

Not imbeciles, then, but certainly not without folly. Wherein does the folly of Bouvard and Pécuchet lie? In part their error is the same as that of their prototype, Monsieur Jourdain—they want to learn too quickly. They do not know the true mode of thought; they have no patience. They would not understand what many of the great researchers meant when they said that they stared at the facts until the facts spoke to them. They are committed to the life of the mind in general, but not, in the way of the true scholar, in particular. They are perhaps too thoroughly Whole Men; they lack the degree of benign limitation which permits an intense preoccupation, making a single subject seem the satisfaction of the demands of a whole temperament. And then we must remember their age; they are forty-seven when they begin, they have no time for patience—they are about the same age as Faust was when he expressed his sense of the inadequacy of all the disciplines. They are Faustian; they must try everything, and to no intellectual moment are they able to say their *"Verweile doch!"*

But their measure of folly is not what makes Bouvard and Pécuchet comic characters. They are comic through the operation of the censorship which the race exercises over those who address themselves to the large enterprises of the spirit. This censorship undertakes to say who is to be allowed to engage upon what high adventures. It decides who, by reason of age or degree of pulchritude or social class, may fall in love, or have surpassing ambitions, or think great thoughts. Whether or not we are ourselves engaged in any of the great spiritual enterprises, we feel it our duty to protect their decorum and their *décor* by laughing at anyone who does not conform to the right image of the lover, the hero, or the thinker. This would be a more disagreeable human trait than in fact it is if we were not at the same time prepared to discover that some of the people whom we debar from their desires have their own special virtues. Leopold Bloom, although he has no ashplant and no irony and does not answer every question "quietly" as Stephen Dedalus does, but, on the contrary, is without dignity in love or thought, is yet seen to be a proper object of our respect and affection. Don Quixote is too old, too stringy, too poor, as well as too late in the day, for chivalry and courtly love, but he is not too much or too little of anything to be wise with a new kind of wisdom. The ancient inscription that Mr. Pickwick discovers is deciphered to read "Bill Stubbs, his mark," which he believes to be nothing but the operation of malice—he really has no mind at all except what makes him defy Dodson & Fogg and become the saint of the Fleet.

So with Bouvard and Pécuchet. They are funny because they are what they are: because they are middle-aged; because one is fat and one is thin; because they wear strange garments; because they are unmarried and awkward in love; because they are innocent; because they are clumsy and things blow up in their faces, or fall on them, or trip them up; because they are gullible and think they are shrewd; because they are full of enthusiasm. Being funny in themselves, being comically *not* the men for high enterprises, they are therefore funny when they undertake the intellectual life. Their comicality is *a priori,* it does not grow out of their lack of intelligence. When it comes to intelligence, many a man has less who can command a better laboratory technique than theirs. Granted that they begin each adventure in stupidity, as they progress through the intellectual disciplines these "simple, lucid, mediocre" minds (as Maupassant called them) are likely to see whatever absurdities are to be seen; they are the catalysts of the foolishness of others.

Then, whether or not they are properly to be called apostles, their degree of virtue and their generosity of spirit are unmistakable. Their hearts—and what is more, their minds—instinctively take the side of the insulted and injured. If they cannot stay long with one idea, they nevertheless live by the mind; the courage that this requires they abundantly have. It is not they who exemplify the vices of the bourgeoisie that Flaubert despised. For the bourgeoisie they have nothing but contempt. In their conflicts with the local priest, doctor, mayor, magnate, it is they who are in the right of things. They stand for intelligence: they are traitors to their class. And they suffer the consequences; they acquire the peculiar pathos of their dedication.

> The evidence of their superiority gave umbrage. As they upheld immoral points of view, they were surely immoral themselves; slanders were invented about them.
>
> Then a pitiable faculty developed in their spirit, that of perceiving stupidity and no longer tolerating it.
>
> Insignificant things made them sad: advertisements in the newspapers, a smug profile, a foolish remark heard by chance.
>
> Musing on what was said in the village, and on there existing as far as the Antipodes [other people like the members of the village bourgeoisie], they felt as though the heaviness of all the earth were weighing on them.

It is no wonder that more than one critic has considered whether Bouvard and Pécuchet must not be taken as standing for Flaubert himself, or for Flaubert and the good friend and neighbor of his later years, Laporte, who found pleasure in helping accumulate the material for *Bouvard and Pécuchet*.

## [ 3 ]

Bouvard and Pécuchet, then, are not the objects of Flaubert's satire. At most they are the butts of his humor, which is strongly qualified by affection. They are never represented as doing anything in the least ignoble or mean. They are "justified" characters. We therefore naturally suppose that the savageness which the book was intended to express is to be found in the exposition of the studies which the two friends undertake—this surely will constitute the fierce indictment of the bourgeois democracy.

But again our supposition is disappointed. The horrors of the culture of the bourgeois democracy play a considerably smaller part than we anticipate. They are less horrible than we had expected. And the animus with which they are exhibited turns out to be not nearly so savage as we had been led to hope.

As I have said, a good many of the misadventures of Bouvard and Pécuchet befall them simply because they are comic characters, or because life is as it is. If their tenant farmer cheats them, if their handyman diddles them, we cannot conclude that rural cupidity and the unreliability of rural labor have been brought about by the ascendancy of the bourgeoisie. If Bouvard, in two wonderful scenes, witnesses the terrible power of sexuality, in human beings and in peacocks, and cannot himself go much further in the direction of passion than a warm flush of inclination, or if Pécuchet contracts gonorrhea from his first sexual experience, we are not exactly being given examples of the effect of the bourgeois swinishness. When the hailstorm destroys the fruit which the two beginners have been almost successful in bringing to maturity, the phenomenon is not cultural but meteorological and, in its context, cosmological. That the agricultural treatises differ from each other, that "as regards marl, Puvis recommends it, Roret's handbook opposes it," this cannot fairly be ascribed to the contemporary corruption of mind—it is of the immemorial nature of farming: since the time of Cain, farmers have exercised their moral faculties on just such differences of opinion. Pécuchet meditates on the inherent contradictions that seem to exist between fruit and branch: "The authorities recommend stopping all the ducts. If not, the sap is injured, and the tree, of course, suffers. For it to flourish, it would have to bear no fruit at all. Yet those that are never pruned or manured yield fruit, smaller, indeed, but better flavored"—this is not an indictment of the stupidity of bourgeois-democratic pomology but a profound consideration of the nature of life, cultural as well as arboricultural. In their true goodness of heart the two friends undertake to rear and educate a pair of brutalized waifs; they fail not because their educational methods are contemptible but because the human material has become intractable.

A considerable part of the intellectual criticism of the novel depends upon the inversion of the snobbish censorship to which I have referred. This is the mode of comedy, which perceives that if any abstruse discipline is confronted with an actual human being, no matter how stupid—and, indeed, the stupider the better —it is the person who is justified as against the discipline. A draper should not be adept in arms nor study the arts of logic or language; still, when put in company of the fencing master who can kill a man by demonstrative reason, or the rhetorician who shows him that $A$ is sounded with the mouth *so,* Monsieur Jourdain is not the greatest fool on the stage, nor would he be if he had secured Aristotle as his teacher. In any vaudeville dialectic the intellectual advantage always rests with the obtuse or primitive person; the straight man, the patient teacher who believes in the subject, is always discredited. No discipline which is confronted with the simplicity, the intellectual *innocence,* of Bouvard and Pécuchet can long maintain its pretense to value.

Then we must have in mind the large part that is played in the book by intellectual and quasi-intellectual absurdities which are as ridiculous as we want to call them, but about which it is impossible for a sensible man to be seriously troubled. Two of the amusing episodes of the novel concern themselves with Bouvard and Pécuchet training their memories by a compound of three mnemonic systems and hardening their bodies according to Amoros's manual of gymnastics. René Descharmes, in his well-known work, *Autour de Bouvard et Pécuchet,* devotes a long chapter to one of the mnemonic systems, the most famous one of all, that of Feinagle, and he gives another chapter to the gymnastic manual. In Descharmes, as in Flaubert, the books are very funny. But we can scarcely believe that these books, and the treatises on hygiene and diet, were the kind of thing that was making Flaubert "rabid." As long as there have been printed books there have been mnemonic systems and they have been absurd; there have always been professors of physical training and they have always had a grandiose solemnity which may still be observed. Quackery is pretty constant in culture, and it is the detritus of culture, not its essence.

An American scholar and critic, Hugh Kenner, recently described *Bouvard and Pécuchet* as "the book into which Flaubert emptied his voluminous notes on human gullibility, groundless learning, *opinions chic,* contradictory authorities, ridiculous enthusiasms, the swill of the 19th century." But we must think with a certain tenderness of some of "the swill of the 19th century" because it has served as the intellectual aliment of certain of the best poets of our age, the men whom we most readily exempt from our general condemnation of our own culture and who have done most to make us aware of the awfulness of our culture and that of the nineteenth century. When Bouvard and Pécuchet involve themselves with the study of psychic and occult phenomena, their researches are no doubt less profound than those of William Butler Yeats, but not different in kind; and although they fall short of Yeats's degree of success in practice, still, on one occasion, they do startle themselves, their audience, and the reader by demonstrating an actual example of clairvoyance. Nothing that the delightful Robert Graves tells us about the Druids contradicts what Bouvard and Pécuchet discover in their study of the science of Celtic archaeology: "Some uttered prophecies, others chanted, others taught botany, medicine, history and literature: in short, all the arts of their epoch. Pythagoras and Plato were their pupils. They instructed the Greeks in metaphysics, the Persians in sorcery, the Etruscans in augury, and the Romans in plating copper and trading in ham." Then the passion of Bouvard and Pécuchet for antiquities, their lust for old documents, and the cultural conclusions they base on their investigations and accumulations are no different from those of Ezra Pound, about whom Mr. Kenner has written so well; and they have Mr. Pound's responsiveness to comprehensive schemes of social and economic reform. Their knowledge of the emotions of the Waste Land is no less intense than that of T. S. Eliot, and based on a not dissimilar experience; with them as with him despair arises from culture and leads to religion.

Readers of literary bent, who have as an element of their pathos the belief that they are persecuted by science,[3] will set special store by those parts of the novel that have the effect of exposing the arrogance as well as the contradictions and absurdities of the

---

[3] It is not sufficiently understood that men of science have an analogous—homologous?—pathos to support them in their own troubles: they believe that they are systematically persecuted by the humanities.

physical science of the day. Everyone who has ever studied literature knows that physical science was the basis of the vulgar materialism of the nineteenth century. In this regard it is well to remember that Flaubert had no principled hostility to science as such—quite to the contrary, indeed. He takes note of the ridiculous statements that science can make, but much of the confusion that Bouvard and Pécuchet experience is the result of their own ineptitude or ignorance rather than of the inadequacy of science itself. It is not the fault of botany—although it may be the fault of a particular elementary textbook of botany—that they believe that all flowers have a pericarp, but look in vain for it when confronted by buttercups and wild strawberry.

Medicine, of course, is the natural prey of the comic—the treatment it receives in *Bouvard and Pécuchet* adds nothing in point of comic method to the classic one established by Molière. And this can serve to remind us of the extent to which the seventeenth and eighteenth centuries figure in the novel. These have become sacred eras, and persons of sensibility believe that either of them can show a virtue for every vice of the nineteenth century. Yet Flaubert represents them as the seedbed of literary stupidity.

> *Think of devices which can captivate,*

says Boileau.

By what means think of these devices?

> *In all your speeches passion should be found,*
> *Go seek the heart, and warm it till it bound.*

How "warm the heart"?

The rules are not enough; genius is also necessary.

And genius is not enough. Corneille, according to the Académie Française, understands nothing of the theatre. Geoffroy depreciated Voltaire. Racine was jeered at by Subligny. Laharpe bellowed at the name of Shakespeare.

What we may call the primary or elemental religious experience of Bouvard and Pécuchet is treated by Flaubert with considerable seriousness and sympathy; it is the theological developments which follow upon that experience that he mocks. This theology cannot be said to be peculiar to the nineteenth century or to the bourgeois democracy.

Again, when it comes to philosophy, it is not merely the philosophy of the nineteenth century that brings Bouvard and Pécuchet to their despair. It is philosophy in general, what anyone except a logical positivist would say were the genuine problems of philosophy. These take, it is true, a specifically modern form, in part because Flaubert had had his say about ancient philosophy in *The Temptation of St. Anthony*. But they go back at least as far as the seventeenth century. "The famous *cogito* bores me," says Bouvard, just like any truthful person who has read Descartes. He and Pécuchet attempt Spinoza. They feel that "all this was like being in a balloon at night, in glacial coldness, carried on an endless voyage towards a bottomless abyss, and with nothing near but the unseizable, the motionless, the eternal. It was too much. They gave it up." As who does not? Their response to the *Ethics* is not foolish, not trivial; they have caught most accurately the emotion that Spinoza enforces upon us, and they know that it is impossible to live with. Yet Flaubert, at the time of writing the novel, had a devoted admiration for Spinoza, as we all have.

What is being mocked? For even literature, the great palladium of Flaubert's life, is not proof against the corrosive action of the simple, lucid, mediocre minds of Bouvard and Pécuchet. It is not merely bad literature that bores them after their first afflatus of enthusiasm; it is literature itself. The elements of each author that at first enchant them—the tone, the idiom, the system of distortion and extravagance—come to be the ground of their eventual boredom. It should perhaps be observed that their experience of literature does not include the very greatest writers, those to whom Flaubert gave his ultimate admiration, Shakespeare, Rabelais, Montaigne, etc. They do, however, read the modern authors for whom Flaubert had great admiration—Balzac, George Sand, Victor Hugo. And who would wish to be so pious as to say that boredom cannot attend our experience of even the very greatest writers?

The more we consider *Bouvard and Pécuchet,* the less the novel can be thought of as nothing but an attack on the culture of the nineteenth century. Bourgeois democracy merely affords the setting for a situation in which it becomes possible to reject culture itself. The novel does nothing less than that: it rejects culture. The human mind experiences the massed accumulation of its own works, those that are traditionally held to be its greatest glories as well as those that are obviously of a contemptible sort, and arrives at the understanding that none will serve its purpose, that all are weariness and vanity, that the whole vast structure of human thought and creation are alien from the human person. Descharmes concludes his study of *Bouvard and Pécuchet* with the statement that the import of the novel is comprehended in a verse from Ecclesiastes which Flaubert might well have used as an epigraph: "And I set my mind to search and investigate through wisdom everything that is done beneath the heavens. It is an evil task that God has given the sons of men with which to occupy themselves." The relevance of the pessimism of Ecclesiastes goes well beyond this single text.

The pessimism of *Bouvard and Pécuchet* is comparable with, although not the same as, that of *Gulliver's Travels.* Just as we may not lessen the depth of the pessimism of *Gulliver's Travels* by reading the book as if it were only Swift's response to the eighteenth century, so we may not lessen the depth of the pessimism of *Bouvard and Pécuchet* by reading it as if it were only Flaubert's response to the nineteenth century.

What does permit us to qualify the pessimism of *Bouvard and Pécuchet* is the comic mode in which it has its existence. The book is genuinely funny, and the comic nature of the two heroes invites us to stand at a certain distance from their woe. We are not dealing with, say, Musset's Octave, he who so advertised his self-pity by calling his history that of "a child of the century," by which he invites the reader to acknowledge a common paternity and thus approve his self-commiseration. Bouvard and Pécuchet permit us to laugh at ourselves in them and yet to remain detached from their plight. They are a *reductio ad absurdum* of our lives in culture, but we are not constrained to follow the reduction as far as it can take us.

They themselves qualify the pessimism of the book by their last act. Another famous copying clerk, an American, Melville's Bartleby the Scrivener, with the classic American pessimism which is more entire than any that the French have contrived, when he perceives the nothingness of society, simply curls up and wills to die, and dies. But when all is lost to Bouvard and Pécuchet, all is not lost: they procure the double copying desk, and the order of the day, which had come to them like a revelation, is *"Copier comme autrefois."* And so we last see them in the metamorphosis to which their lives entitle them, a sort of bachelor Baucis and Philemon, rustling their leaves at each other with a sweet papery sound. They have discovered the *"travailler sans raisonner,"* the virtue of work without philosophizing, which *Candide* inculcates. Yet the abrogation of abstruse research does not mean the abrogation of mind, for what they copy from the old papers which they indiscriminately buy are the absurdities they have learned to recognize. The results of their copying are to constitute, according to Flaubert's plan, the last part of the novel. Scholars have debated which of Flaubert's several collections of absurdities was to appear as the fruit of their efforts. The weight of the evidence seems to give that place to *The Dictionary of Accepted Ideas,* and most readers will be willing to accept this conclusion if only because of the pleasures of the *Dictionary* itself, which is the most elaborate of the collections.[4] But for the understanding of the novel itself it is almost enough to know that *something* was to follow, that, reduced as the two friends are, they have not lost their love of mind, to which they testify by recording the mind's failures.

## [ 4 ]

The pessimism of *Bouvard and Pécuchet* is qualified by certain other considerations. These are extraneous to the text, but our sense of the ambiguity of the novel justifies us in going beyond the text to see if we may gain further understanding from an awareness of the circumstances of its composition. Indeed, it is virtually impossible not to do something of this sort. In the time between his death and his centenary in 1921 the fame of Flaubert increased to the point where he was a classic of his language and the subject of an elaborate scholarship. His novels, which he had written according to his famous ideal of strict objectivity and stern impersonality, were read—and even when there was no excuse of ambiguity—more and more in the light of his personal legend, which seemed to grow ever greater in its power of appeal.

If there is such a thing as biographical success, Flaubert

[4] The *Dictionary* may now be read in Jacques Barzun's translation, published by New Directions.

achieved it in its fullest measure, for the last period of his life is as interesting, in both event and thought, as the early years in which his mind was formed and the middle years of his decisive productions; and its pathos is irresistible. This pathos, I venture to suppose, is similar in the effect it has upon the French reader to that which moves the English reader in the life of Swift. It is the pathos of the man whose savage pride induces him to have always before his mind the idea of mankind as a whole, and to regard the human actuality with an angry disgust so intense that it seems to him—and sometimes to others—like a madness. Those individuals whom he exempts from his general contempt for the human kind he grapples to himself with hoops of steel. If he is incapable of marriage and even of sexual love in any conventional sense, he can give to a few women an extreme devotion; and to many men he can give a friendship of surpassing respect and loyalty.

It was in his remarkably deep affections that Flaubert was struck again and again in his last years. "I am obsessed by the dead (my dead)," he wrote to Laure de Maupassant. "Is this a sign of old age? I think so." He was fifty-three. The year was 1873 and the necrology of the last four years had been long; many losses were still to come. His mother, his dearest friends, his literary colleagues and comrades-in-arms—their deaths accumulated and were augmented by the passing of people whom he did not love as he loved his mother, or George Sand, or Louis Bouilhet, or whom he did not respect as he did Jules de Goncourt, or Gautier, or even Sainte-Beuve, but who nevertheless embodied his past, such as Louise Colet, his former mistress, and Maurice Schlesinger, the husband of the woman Flaubert had loved with a virtually mystic passion since his adolescence and whom he had enshrined as the Mme. Arnoux of *A Sentimental Education*.

He could make of his life an altar of the dead, as witness the time, effort, and passion he gave to keep alive the memory of the cherished Louis Bouilhet. But he could also make it an altar of the living. Perhaps he would not have said with Henry James that life is nothing unless it is sacrificial, but he acted as if he believed this to be so when he offered up his independence for the happiness of his niece Caroline.

Caroline Commanville was the only child of Flaubert's only sister, who had died in 1846, and she had been reared by her grandmother and her uncle. To Caro, as she was called, Flaubert gave the full of the devotion of which he was capable. His love, characteristically enough, expressed itself in his solicitude for the grace of her mind. Something of his yearning tenderness for her, which appears so unabashedly in the letters which she published after his death, was lent to Bouvard and Pécuchet when, moved in part by belated parental impulses, they adopt the stray children to educate them for decorous and useful lives. Flaubert spent thirteen years on Caro's education, and the goal of his affectionate efforts was like that of Nature in Wordsworth's poem:

> This Child I to myself shall take;
> She shall be mine, and I shall make
> A Lady of my own

—a Lady who in her own person should be the answer to the vulgarity and stupidity of the time.

How far he did indeed succeed in his best hopes for the intellectual grace of Caro may be judged by American readers from the description of her which Willa Cather gives after meeting her at a hotel at Aix in 1930, when she was a woman of eighty-four. And nothing can suggest better the moral limitations of Miss Cather and her feminized universe than the fact that although she renders the most intense and delicate homage to the charm of Mme. Franklin-Grout (as she had become), speaking at length of her manners, her command of many languages, the purity of her passion for art, her friendship with her uncle's great friends, her closeness to her uncle himself, she gives no intimation that for the sake of Caro, and at her behest, Flaubert had put himself into financial jeopardy, surrendering the fortune upon which he depended for his literary life, and with very little thanks from the beneficiary.

Up to 1875 the business affairs of Caroline's husband Commanville seemed to justify an elaborate establishment in Paris and a fashionable and expensive way of life. Then it became clear that Commanville was on the verge of bankruptcy. To save the Commanvilles from disgrace Flaubert pledged his entire fortune—when it came to the bourgeois pieties he was to be outdone by no one. He gave up his pleasant flat in Paris and took cheaper rooms, and in general greatly curtailed his expenses. He sold the property at Deauville from which he derived his income. At one time it seemed probable that he would have to give up the house at Croisset, where he had lived virtually all his life. This horrified him and wrung from him an agonized cry—without it, he said, using the English word, he would have no *home*. George Sand offered to buy it if possible and let him live in it all his life, but the sale proved unnecessary. In all, Flaubert put at the disposal of the Commanvilles 1,200,000 francs, in return for which he was to receive a small allowance.

The full extent of the sacrifice can be properly understood only if we feel the force of Gautier's remark that Flaubert's bourgeois fortune was part of his creative endowment. The sacrifice being what it was, the Commanvilles' subsequent behavior gives the incident a Lear-like character. They did not pay the allowance promptly and Flaubert had to importune for it. They were angry when Flaubert, with much reluctance and humiliation, consented to allow his friends to procure a pension for him; they did not forgive the friends who had won his consent and campaigned for the pension. They felt he was a drain on their resources and called him "the consumer"; their own way of life continued to be expensive. They required him to enlist his friends in further help to them. When the devoted Laporte, who himself had lost his fortune, refused to commit himself further, they insisted that Flaubert break with him, which he did in great sadness.

These events, interesting in themselves, are significant for our purpose as constituting the circumstance in which Flaubert wrote the *Three Tales* and as having a bearing upon their common theme of the sacrifice of the self; and the *Three Tales* must inevitably be read as a gloss upon *Bouvard and Pécuchet*.

In September of 1875, with the Commanville affairs temporarily under control, Flaubert went to spend six weeks at Concarneau with his old friend, the naturalist Georges Pouchet. Flaubert's nerves were in a bad state; he was sadly distraught. He envied the calm with which his scientist friend went about his work. Unable to take up his own work on *Bouvard and Pécuchet*, he swam and walked to restore his equanimity and he began the story of *St. Julian*. He took it with him when he left Concarneau and finished it in January. In February he began *A Simple Heart*, which he completed in August. In August he began *Herodias*, which he finished the following February. The stories appeared as a newspaper serial and then in a volume; they were greeted with almost universal admiration—Flaubert's first popular success since *Madame Bovary*.

The part that these three stories play in Flaubert's artistic development cannot concern us here. Nor can we stop to consider all that they might be understood to say of Flaubert's inner life. What is of immediate consequence to us is the theme which they have in common and how that bears upon *Bouvard and Pécuchet*.

The stories are well known and need be recalled but briefly. All are associated with Flaubert's native Rouen. The legend of St. Julian is the subject of a window of the Cathedral; the Herodias story is told on the tympanum of the Cathedral's south portal. The Félicité of *A Simple Heart* was a servant girl whom Flaubert had known in his boyhood. The story of St. Julian, a Christianized version of the Oedipus legend, tells of a young nobleman brought up to arms and the chase; his passion for killing is exorbitant (the catalogue of the beasts he slays reminds us of nothing so much as the fifteen hundred volumes Flaubert read for *Bouvard and Pécuchet*), until one day it is prophesied to him by a gigantic and invulnerable stag that he will kill his own mother and father. The prophecy comes true despite Julian's best efforts to circumvent it. Julian, shunned by all mankind, lives as a hermit. One cold night there comes to his hut a leper of extreme loathesomeness who asks for food, then for the warmth of Julian's embrace, then for a kiss upon his ghastly mouth. And as Julian's *caritas* extends to this last request, the leper appears as Christ and carries Julian off in glory. *A Simple Heart* is a record of a life of religious piety and of entire devotion to others. Virtually the only events of Félicité's life are the deaths of those whom she loves and serves. (It has been remarked that Félicité has a seizure on the road very much like that which Flaubert suffered as the first episode of his illness; other possible connections with Flaubert are her cherishing of her nephew, her being exploited by her relatives, her being left destitute by the death of her mistress, and her continuing to live by sufferance in the stripped and empty house.) *Herodias* is the story of John the Baptist imprisoned by the Tetrarch Antipas, of Salome's dance, and the severed head.

The religious elements of the three stories must not mislead us about the condition of Flaubert's belief. The *Tales* are not to be thought of as tentatives toward an avowal of faith. For this Flaubert's attitude toward religion was far too complex. Even in *Bouvard and Pécuchet,* as I have noted, Flaubert treats simple, primary religious faith, or impulse to faith, with great gentleness; what dismayed him were the intellectual extrapolations from this simplicity. Yet his response to religion is not comprised by the tenderness he could show to simple faith and his contempt for systematic theology. What his attitude to religion actually was in its considerable complexity has been well described by Philip Spencer in his *Flaubert:* "He seems . . . to have regarded Christianity as a spent force. . . . The only two elements in Catholicism to which Flaubert responded were subordinate to the main tradition and divergent from it: the hatred of life, the negation of life's goodness, which he thought he discovered in Catholic philosophy, and, concomitant with it, the rigorous self-abasement of asceticism. But his own religious feeling, if such it can be called, was diffuse—a kind of creatureliness before the mystery of creation. 'What draws me above all things,' he wrote in 1857, 'is religion. I mean all religions, not one rather than another. Each dogma on its own repels me, but I consider the feeling that created them as the most natural and poetical in humanity. I don't like philosophers who find there only fraud and foolishness.' " A man who can speak thus does not easily "turn to" religion, and the *Three Tales* must not be thought of even as the tribute to religion of an unbeliever who perceives the charms and advantages of faith and who regrets his inability to believe. Flaubert was a very serious man.

But we shall not be wrong if we think of the stories as a tribute to what Flaubert took to be a characteristic mode of Christianity, the "negation of life's goodness"—life's goodness in general and specifically the goodness of man's life in culture. In each of the stories the protagonist exists beyond the life in culture and stands divested of every garment that culture weaves. Julian passes beyond parental love, beyond social rank, beyond heroism and fame, beyond the domestic affections, beyond all the things, persons, and institutions that bind us to the earth, and he reaches that moment of charity which is the surrender of what Flaubert believed to be the richest luxury of culture, the self in the separateness of sensibility and pride that define it. Félicité, endowed by nature and culture with no other gift than that of the power to love and serve, is deprived of every person upon whom her love has fixed and is left with no other object to cherish than her poor stuffed parrot, the dumb effigy of the Speaking Bird, the Logos, the Holy Ghost. John the Baptist, naked and solitary, cries out from his prison-pit against the court of Antipas, and Flaubert is at his usual pains to specify not only the deeds but the artifacts—the garments and the food and the armament hidden beneath the palace—of which the Baptist's naked and solitary voice is the negation.

The *Tales,* that is, continue Flaubert's old despair of culture, which was, we may say, the prime condition of his art; it was a despair which was the more profound, we need scarcely say, because it was the issue of so great a hope. Emma Bovary had tried to live by the promises of selfhood which culture had seemed to make, and culture had destroyed her. Frédéric Moreau had ruined himself by never quite believing in the selfhood which culture cherishes as its dearest gift. Now Flaubert considers the condition of the spirit which puts itself as far as possible beyond the promises, the consolations, and the demands of culture; in each of the *Three Tales* he asks what remains when culture is rejected and transcended. The answer, given with a notable firmness and simplicity, is that something of highest value does remain—it is the self affirmed in self-denial: life is nothing unless sacrificial. And Bouvard and Pécuchet, sitting at their double copying desk, having a work and each other, but stripped of every idea, every theory, every shred of culture beyond what is necessary to keep men alive and still human, are, in their own mild negation of self, intended by Flaubert to be among the company of his saints.

# Mansfield Park

SOONER or later, when we speak of Jane Austen, we speak of her irony, and it is better to speak of it sooner rather than later because nothing can so far mislead us about her work as a wrong understanding of this one aspect of it. Most people either value irony too much or fear it too much. This is true of their response to irony in its first simple meaning, that of a device of rhetoric by which we say one thing and intend its opposite, or intend more, or less, than we say. It is equally true of their response to irony in its derived meaning, the loose generalized sense in which we speak of irony as a quality of someone's mind, Montaigne's for example. Both the excessive valuation and the excessive fear of irony lead us to misconceive the part it can play in the intellectual and moral life. To Jane Austen, irony does not mean, as it means to many, a moral detachment or the tone of superiority that goes with moral detachment. Upon irony so conceived she has made her own judgment in the figure of Mr. Bennet of *Pride and Prejudice,* whose irony of moral detachment is shown to be the cause of his becoming a moral nonentity.

Jane Austen's irony is only secondarily a matter of tone. Primarily it is a method of comprehension. It perceives the world through an awareness of its contradictions, paradoxes, and anomalies. It is by no means detached. It is partisan with generosity of spirit—it is on the side of "life," of "affirmation." But it is preoccupied not only with the charm of the expansive virtues but also with the cost at which they are to be gained and exercised. This cost is regarded as being at once ridiculously high and perfectly fair. What we may call Jane Austen's first or basic irony is the recognition of the fact that spirit is not free, that it is conditioned, that it is limited by circumstance. This, as everyone knows from childhood on, is indeed an anomaly. Her next and consequent irony, has reference to the fact that only by reason of this anomaly does spirit have virtue and meaning.

In irony, even in the large derived sense of the word, there is a kind of malice. The ironist has the intention of practicing upon the misplaced confidence of the literal mind, of disappointing comfortable expectation. Jane Austen's malice of irony is directed not only upon certain of the characters of her novels but also upon the reader himself. We are quick, too quick, to understand that *Northanger Abbey* invites us into a snug conspiracy to disabuse the little heroine of the errors of her corrupted fancy—Catherine Morland, having become addicted to novels of terror, has accepted their inadmissible premise, she believes that life is violent and unpredictable. And that is exactly what life is shown to be by the events of the story: it is we who must be disabused of our belief that life is sane and orderly. The shock of our surprise at the disappointment of our settled views is of course the more startling because we believe that we have settled our views in conformity with the author's own. Just when we have concluded in *Sense and Sensibility* that we ought to prefer Elinor Dashwood's sense to Marianne Dashwood's sensibility, Elinor herself yearns toward the anarchic passionateness of sensibility. In *Emma* the heroine is made to stand at bay to our adverse judgment through virtually the whole novel, but we are never permitted to close in for the kill—some unnamed quality in the girl, some trait of vivacity or will, erects itself into a moral principle, or at least a vital principle, and frustrates our moral blood-lust.

This interference with our moral and intellectual comfort constitutes, as I say, a malice on the part of the author. And when we respond to Jane Austen with pleasure, we are likely to do so in part because we recognize in her work an analogue with the malice of the experienced universe, with the irony of circumstance, which is always disclosing more than we bargained for.

But there is one novel of Jane Austen's, *Mansfield Park,* in which the characteristic irony seems not to be at work. Indeed, one might say of this novel that it undertakes to discredit irony and to affirm literalness, that it demonstrates that there are no two ways about anything. And *Mansfield Park* is for this reason held by many to be the novel that is least representative of Jane Austen's peculiar attractiveness. For those who admire her it is likely to make an occasion for embarrassment. By the same token, it is the novel which the depreciators of Jane Austen may cite most tellingly in justification of their antagonism.

About this antagonism a word must be said. Few writers have been the object of an admiration so fervent as that which is given to Jane Austen. At the same time, she has been the object of great dislike. Lord David Cecil has said that the people who do not like Jane Austen are the kind of people "who do not like sunshine and unselfishness," and Dr. Chapman, the distinguished editor of Jane Austen's novels and letters, although dissenting from Lord David's opinion, has speculated that perhaps "a certain lack of charity" plays a part in the dislike. But Mark Twain, to take but one example, manifestly did not lack charity or dislike sunshine and unselfishness, and Mark Twain

said of Jane Austen that she inspired in him an "animal repugnance." The personal intensity of both parties to the dispute will
serve to suggest how momentous, how elemental, is the issue
that Jane Austen presents.

The *animality* of Mark Twain's repugnance is probably to
be taken as the male's revulsion from a society in which women
seem to be at the center of interest and power, as a man's panic
fear at a fictional world in which the masculine principle, although represented as admirable and necessary, is prescribed
and controlled by a female mind. Professor Garrod, whose essay,
"Jane Austen, A Depreciation," is a *summa* of all the reasons
for disliking Jane Austen, expresses a repugnance which is very
nearly as feral as Mark Twain's; he implies that a direct sexual
insult is being offered to men by a woman author who "describes
everything in the youth of women which does not matter" in
such a way as to appeal to "that age in men when they have
begun to ask themselves whether anything matters." The sexual
protest is not only masculine—Charlotte Brontë despised Jane
Austen for representing men and women as nothing but ladies
and gentlemen.

The sexual objection to Jane Austen is a very common one,
even when it is not made explicit. It is not valid, yet it ought
to be taken seriously into account. But then there is Emerson
with his characteristic sexual indifference, his striking lack of
animality, and Emerson's objection to Jane Austen is quick
and entire, is instinctual. He says that she is "sterile" and goes on
to call her "vulgar." Emerson held this opinion out of his passion
of concern for the liberty of the self and the autonomy of spirit,
and his holding it must make us see that the sexual reason for
disliking Jane Austen must be subsumed under another reason
which is larger, and, actually, even more elemental: the fear of
imposed constraint. Dr. Chapman says something of this sort

when he speaks of "political prejudice" and "impatient idealism" as perhaps having something to do with the dislike of Jane Austen. But these phrases, apart from the fact that they prejudge the case, do not suggest the biological force of the resistance which certain temperaments offer to the idea of society as a limiting condition of the individual spirit.

Such temperaments are not likely to take Jane Austen's irony as a melioration of her particular idea of society. On the contrary, they are likely to suppose that irony is but the engaging manner by which she masks society's crude coercive power. And they can point to *Mansfield Park* to show what the social coercion is in all its literal truth, before irony has beglamoured us about it and induced us to be comfortable with it—here it is in all its negation, in all the force of its repressiveness. Perhaps no other work of genius has ever spoken, or seemed to speak, so insistently for cautiousness and constraint, even for dullness. No other great novel has so anxiously asserted the need to find security, to establish, in fixity and enclosure, a refuge from the dangers of openness and chance.

There is scarcely one of our modern pieties that it does not offend. Despite our natural tendency to permit costume and manners to separate her world from ours, most readers have no great difficulty in realizing that all the other novels of Jane Austen are, in essential ways, of our modern time. This is the opinion of the many students with whom I have read the novels; not only do the young men controvert by their enthusiasm the judgment of Professor Garrod that Jane Austen appeals only to men of middle age, but they easily and naturally assume her to have a great deal to say to them about the modern personality. But *Mansfield Park* is the exception, and it is bitterly resented. It scandalizes the modern assumptions about social relations, about virtue, about religion, sex, and art. Most troubling of all is its preference for rest over motion. To deal with the world by condemning it, by withdrawing from it and shutting it out, by making oneself and one's mode and principles of life the very center of existence and to live the round of one's days in the stasis and peace thus contrived—this, in an earlier age, was one of the recognized strategies of life, but to us it seems not merely impracticable but almost wicked.

Yet *Mansfield Park* is a great novel, its greatness being commensurate with its power to offend.

*Mansfield Park* was published in 1814, only one year after the publication of *Pride and Prejudice,* and no small part of its interest derives from the fact that it seems to controvert everything that its predecessor tells us about life. One of the striking things about *Pride and Prejudice* is that it achieves a quality of transcendence through comedy. The comic mode typically insists upon the fact of human limitation, even of human littleness, but *Pride and Prejudice* makes comedy reverse itself and yield the implication of a divine enlargement. The novel celebrates the traits of spiritedness, vivacity, celerity, and lightness, and associates them with happiness and virtue. Its social doctrine is a generous one, asserting the right of at least the *good* individual to define himself according to his own essence. It is animated by an impulse to forgiveness. One understands very easily why many readers are moved to explain their pleasure in the book by reference to Mozart, especially *The Marriage of Figaro.*

Almost the opposite can be said of *Mansfield Park.* Its impulse is not to forgive but to condemn. Its praise is not for social freedom but for social stasis. It takes full notice of spiritedness, vivacity, celerity, and lightness, but only to reject them as having nothing to do with virtue and happiness, as being, indeed, deterrents to the good life.

Nobody, I believe, has ever found it possible to like the heroine of *Mansfield Park*. Fanny Price is overtly virtuous and consciously virtuous. Our modern literary feeling is very strong against people who, when they mean to be virtuous, believe they know how to reach their goal and do reach it. We think that virtue is not interesting, even that it is not really virtue, unless it manifests itself as a product of "grace" operating through a strong inclination to sin. Our favorite saint is likely to be Augustine; he is sweetened for us by his early transgressions. We cannot understand how any age could have been interested in Patient Griselda. We admire Milton only if we believe with Blake that he was of the Devil's party, of which we are fellow travelers; the paradox of the *felix culpa* and the "fortunate fall" appeals to us for other than theological reasons and serves to validate all sins and all falls, which we take to be the signs of life.

It does not reconcile us to the virtue of Fanny Price that it is rewarded by more than itself. The shade of Pamela hovers over her career. We take failure to be the mark of true virtue and we do not like it that, by reason of her virtue, the terrified little stranger in Mansfield Park grows up to be virtually its mistress.

Even more alienating is the state of the heroine's health. Fanny is in a debilitated condition through the greater part of the novel. At a certain point the author retrieves this situation and sees to it that Fanny becomes taller, prettier, and more energetic. But the first impression remains of a heroine who cannot cut a basket of roses without fatigue and headache.

Fanny's debility becomes the more striking when we consider that no quality of the heroine of *Pride and Prejudice* is more appealing than her physical energy. We think of Elizabeth Bennet as in physical movement; her love of dancing confirms our belief that she moves gracefully. It is characteristic of her to smile; she likes to tease; she loves to talk. She is remarkably responsive to all attractive men. And to outward seeming, Mary Crawford of *Mansfield Park* is another version of Elizabeth Bennet, and Mary Crawford is the antithesis of Fanny Price. The boldness with which the antithesis is contrived is typical of the uncompromising honesty of *Mansfield Park*. Mary Crawford is conceived—is calculated—to win the charmed admiration of almost any reader. She is all pungency and wit. Her mind is as lively and competent as her body; she can bring not only a horse but a conversation to the gallop. She is downright, open, intelligent, impatient. Irony is her natural mode, and we are drawn to think of her voice as being as nearly the author's own as Elizabeth Bennet's is. Yet in the end we are asked to believe that she is not to be admired, that her lively mind compounds, by very reason of its liveliness, with the world, the flesh, and the devil.

This strange, this almost perverse, rejection of Mary Crawford's vitality in favor of Fanny's debility lies at the very heart of the novel's intention. "The divine," said T. E. Hulme in *Speculations,* "is not life at its intensest. It contains in a way an almost anti-vital element." Perhaps it cannot quite be said that "the divine" is the object of Fanny's soul, yet she is a Christian heroine. Hulme expresses with an air of discovery what was once taken for granted in Christian feeling. Fanny is one of the poor in spirit. It is not a condition of the soul to which we are nowadays sympathetic. We are likely to suppose that it masks hostility—many modern readers respond to Fanny by suspecting her. This is perhaps not unjustified, but as we try to understand what Jane Austen meant by the creation of such a heroine, we must have in mind the tradition which affirmed the peculiar sanctity of the sick, the weak, and the dying. The tradition perhaps came to an end for literature with the death of Milly Theale, the heroine of Henry James's *The Wings of the Dove,* but

Dickens exemplifies its continuing appeal in the nineteenth century, and it was especially strong in the eighteenth century. Clarissa's sickness and death confirm her Christian virtue, and in Fielding's *Amelia,* the novel which may be said to bear the same relation to *Tom Jones* that *Mansfield Park* bears to *Pride and Prejudice,* the sign of the heroine's Christian authority is her loss of health and beauty.

Fanny is a Christian heroine: it is therefore not inappropriate that the issue between her and Mary Crawford should be concentrated in the debate over whether or not Edmund Bertram shall become a clergyman. We are not, however, from our reading of the novel, inclined to say more than that the debate is "not inappropriate"—it startles us to discover that ordination was what Jane Austen said her novel was to be "about." In the letter in which she tells of having received the first copies of *Pride and Prejudice,* and while she is still in high spirits over her achievement, she says, "Now I will try and write something else, and it shall be a complete change of subject—ordination." A novelist, of course, presents a new subject to himself, or to his friends, in all sorts of ways that are inadequate to his real intention as it eventually will disclose itself—the most unsympathetic reader of *Mansfield Park* would scarcely describe it as being about ordination. Yet the question of ordination is of essential importance to the novel.

It is not really a religious question, but, rather, a cultural question, having to do with the meaning and effect of a *profession.* Two senses of that word are in point here, the open avowal of principles and beliefs as well as a man's commitment to a particular kind of life work. It is the latter sense that engages us first. The argument between Fanny and Mary is over what will happen to Edmund as a person, as a *man,* if he chooses to become a clergyman. To Mary, every clergyman is the Mr.

Collins of *Pride and Prejudice;* she thinks of ordination as a surrender of manhood. But Fanny sees the Church as a career that claims a man's best manly energies; her expressed view of the churchman's function is that which was to develop through the century, exemplified in, say, Thomas Arnold, who found the Church to be an adequate field for what he called his talents for command.

The matter of a man's profession was of peculiar importance to Jane Austen. It weighs heavily against Mr. Bennet that, his estate being entailed, he has made no effort to secure his family against his death, and by reason of his otiosity he is impotent to protect his family's good name from the consequences of Lydia's sexual escapade. He is represented as being not only less a man but also as less a gentleman than his brother-in-law Gardiner, who is in trade in London. Jane Austen's feelings about men in relation to their profession reach their highest intensity in *Persuasion,* in the great comic scene in which Sir Walter Elliot is flattered by Mrs. Clay's telling him that every profession puts its mark upon a man's face, and that a true gentleman will avoid this vulgar injury to his complexion. And in the same novel much is made of the professional pride of the Navy and the good effect it has upon the personal character.

In nineteenth-century England the ideal of professional commitment inherits a large part of the moral prestige of the ideal of the gentleman. Such figures as the engineer Daniel Doyce of *Little Dorrit* or Dr. Lydgate of *Middlemarch* represent the developing belief that a man's moral life is bound up with his loyalty to the discipline of his calling. The concern with the profession was an aspect of the ethical concept which was prepotent in the spiritual life of England in the nineteenth century, the concept of duty. The Church, in its dominant form and characteristic virtue, was here quite at one with the tendency of secular feeling; its preoccupation may be said to have been less with the achievement of salvation than with the performance of duty.

The word grates upon our moral ear. We do what we should do, but we shrink from giving it the name of duty. "Cooperation," "social-mindedness," the "sense of the group," "class solidarity"—these locutions do not mean what duty means. They have been invented precisely for the purpose of describing right conduct in such a way as *not* to imply what duty implies—a self whose impulses and desires are very strong, and a willingness to subordinate these impulses and desires to the claim of some external nonpersonal good. The new locutions are meant to suggest that right action is typically to be performed without any pain to the self.

The men of the nineteenth century did not imagine this possibility. They thought that morality was terribly hard to achieve, at the cost of renunciation and sacrifice. We of our time often wonder what could have made the difficulty. We wonder, for example, why a man like Matthew Arnold felt it necessary to remind himself almost daily of duty, why he believed that the impulses must be "bridled" and "chained down," why he insisted on the "strain and labour and suffering" of the moral life. We are as much puzzled as touched by the tone in which F. W. H. Myers tells of walking with George Eliot in the Fellows' Garden at Trinity "on an evening of rainy May," and she, speaking of God, Immortality, and Duty, said how inconceivable was the first, how unbelievable the second, "yet how peremptory and absolute the third." "Never, perhaps, have sterner accents affirmed the sovereignty of impersonal and unrecompensing Law. I listened, and night fell; her grave majestic countenance turned towards me like a sybil's in the gloom; it was as though she withdrew from my grasp, one by one, the two scrolls of promise, and left me the third scroll only, awful with inevitable fate." [1]

The diminution of faith in the promise of religion accounts for much but not for all the concern with duty in nineteenth-century England. It was not a crisis of religion that made Wordsworth the laureate of duty. What Wordsworth asks in his great poem "Resolution and Independence" is how the self, in its highest manifestation, in the Poet, can preserve itself from its own nature, from the very sensibility and volatility that define it, from its own potentiality of what Wordsworth calls with superb explicitness "despondency and madness." Something has attenuated the faith in the self of four years before, of "Tintern Abbey," the certitude that "Nature never did betray/ The heart that loved her": a new Paraclete is needed and he comes in the shape of the Old Leech Gatherer, a man rocklike in endurance, rocklike in insensibility, annealed by a simple, rigorous religion, preserved in life and in virtue by the "anti-vital element" and transfigured by that element.

---

[1] But if we are puzzled by the tone of this, we cannot say that it is a tone inappropriate to its subject. The idea of duty was central in the English culture of the nineteenth century, and in general when Englishmen of the period speak about duty *in propria persona* they speak movingly. This makes it all the stranger that when they express the idea through a literary form they scarcely ever do so in an elevated manner. They seem to have thought of duty as an ideal to be associated in literature chiefly with domestic life or with dullness. As a consequence, everyone was delighted with the jig in *Ruddigore:* "For duty, duty must be done,/ The rule applies to everyone./ Unpleasant though that duty be,/ To shirk the task were fiddledeedee." It was left to foreigners to deal with the idea as if it were of *tragic* import. Melville in *Billy Budd* and Vigny in his military stories exploited the moral possibilities of the British naval tradition of Nelson and Collingwood which even Wordsworth had been able to represent only abstractly and moralistically in his "character" of the Happy Warrior; and Conrad is the first English novelist to make the idea of duty large and interesting. It is hard to believe that the moral idea which Emily Dickinson celebrate. in her brilliant poem on Thermopylae and associates with high intelligence is the same idea that Tennyson celebrates in "The Charge of the Light Brigade" and associates with stupidity.

That the self may destroy the self by the very energies that define its being, that the self may be preserved by the negation of its own energies—this, whether or not we agree, makes a paradox, makes an irony, that catches our imagination. Much of the nineteenth-century preoccupation with duty was not a love of law for its own sake, but rather a concern with the hygiene of the self. If we are aware of this, we are prepared to take seriously an incident in *Mansfield Park* that on its face is perfectly absurd.

The great fuss that is made over the amateur theatricals can seem to us a mere travesty on virtue. And the more so because it is never made clear why it is so very wrong for young people in a dull country house to put on a play. The mystery deepens, as does our sense that *Mansfield Park* represents an unusual state of the author's mind, when we know that amateur theatricals were a favorite amusement in Jane Austen's home. The play is Kotzebue's *Lovers' Vows* and it deals with illicit love and a bastard, but Jane Austen, as her letters and novels clearly show, was not a prude. Some of the scenes of the play permit Maria Bertram and Henry Crawford to make love in public, but this is not said to be decisively objectionable. What is decisive is a traditional, almost primitive, feeling about dramatic impersonation. We know of this, of course, from Plato, and it is one of the points on which almost everyone feels superior to Plato, but it may have more basis in actuality than we commonly allow. It is the fear that the impersonation of a bad or inferior character will have a harmful effect upon the impersonator, that, indeed, the impersonation of any other self will diminish the integrity of the real self.

A right understanding of the seemingly absurd episode of the play must dispel any doubt of the largeness of the cultural significance of *Mansfield Park*. The American philosopher George

Mead has observed that the "assumption of roles" was one of the most important elements of Romanticism. Mead conceived of impersonation as a new mode of thought appropriate to that new sense of the self which was Romanticism's characteristic achievement. It was, he said further, the self's method of defining itself. Involved as we all are in this mode of thought and in this method of self-definition, we are not likely to respond sympathetically to Jane Austen when she puts it under attack as being dangerous to the integrity of the self as a moral agent. Yet the testimony of John Keats stands in her support—in one of his most notable letters Keats says of the poet that, as poet, he cannot be a moral agent; he has no "character," no "self," no "identity"; he is concerned not with moral judgment but with "gusto," subordinating his own being to that of the objects of his creative regard. Wordsworth implies something of a related sort when he contrasts the poet's volatility of mood with the bulking permanence of identity of the Old Leech Gatherer. And of course not only the poet but the reader may be said to be involved in the problems of identity and of (in the literal sense) integrity. Literature offers the experience of the diversification of the self, and Jane Austen puts the question of literature at the moral center of her novel.

The massive ado that is organized about the amateur theatricals and the dangers of impersonation thus has a direct bearing upon the matter of Edmund Bertram's profession. The election of a profession is of course in a way the assumption of a role, but it is a permanent impersonation which makes virtually impossible the choice of another. It is a commitment which fixes the nature of the self.

The ado about the play extends its significance still further. It points, as it were, to a great and curious triumph of Jane Austen's art. The triumph consists in this—that although on a first reading of *Mansfield Park* Mary Crawford's speeches are all delightful, they diminish in charm as we read the novel a second time. We begin to hear something disagreeable in their intonation: it is the peculiarly modern bad quality which Jane Austen was the first to represent—insincerity. This is a trait very different from the *hypocrisy* of the earlier novelists. Mary Crawford's intention is not to deceive the world but to comfort herself; she impersonates the woman she thinks she ought to be. And as we become inured to the charm of her performance we see through the moral impersonation and are troubled that it should have been thought necessary. In Mary Crawford we have the first brilliant example of a distinctively modern type, the person who cultivates the *style* of sensitivity, virtue, and intelligence.

Henry Crawford has more sincerity than his sister, and the adverse judgment which the novel makes on him is therefore arrived at with greater difficulty. He is conscious of his charm, of the winningness of his personal style, which has in it—as he knows—a large element of *natural* goodness and generosity. He is no less conscious of his lack of weight and solidity; his intense courtship of Fanny is, we may say, his effort to add the gravity of principle to his merely natural goodness. He becomes, however, the prey to his own charm, and in his cold flirtation with Maria Bertram he is trapped by his impersonation of passion—his role requires that he carry Maria off from a dull marriage to a life of boring concupiscence. It is his sister's refusal to attach any moral importance to this event that is the final proof of her deficiency in seriousness. Our modern impulse to resist the condemnation of sexuality and of sexual liberty cannot properly come into play here, as at first we think it should. For it is not sexuality that is being condemned, but precisely that form of asexuality that incurred D. H. Lawrence's greatest scorn—that is, sexuality as a game, or as a drama, sexuality as an expression of mere will or mere personality, as a sign of power, or prestige, or autonomy: as, in short, an impersonation and an insincerity.

A passage in one of her letters of 1814, written while *Mansfield Park* was in composition, enforces upon us how personally Jane Austen was involved in the question of principle as against personality, of character as against style. A young man has been paying court to her niece Fanny Knight, and the girl is troubled by, exactly, the effect of his principledness on his style. Her aunt's comment is especially interesting because it contains an avowal of sympathy with Evangelicism, an opinion which is the reverse of that which she had expressed in a letter of 1809 and had represented in *Pride and Prejudice,* yet the religious opinion is but incidental to the affirmation that is being made of the moral advantage of the profession of principle, whatever may be its effect on the personal style.

Mr. J. P.—— has advantages which do not often meet in one person. His only fault indeed seems Modesty. If he were less modest, he would be more agreeable, speak louder & look Impudenter;—and is it not a fine Character of which Modesty is the only defect?—I have no doubt that he will get more lively & more like yourselves as he is more with you;—he will catch your ways if he belongs to you. And as to there being any objection from his *Goodness,* from the danger of his becoming even Evangelical, I cannot admit *that.* I am by no means convinced that we ought not all to be Evangelicals, & am at least persuaded that they who are so from Reason and Feeling, must be happiest & safest. Do not be frightened from the connection by your Brothers having most wit. Wisdom is better than Wit, & in the long run will certainly have the laugh on her side; & don't be frightened by the idea of his acting more strictly up to the precepts of the New Testament than others.

The great charm, the charming greatness, of *Pride and Prej-udice* is that it permits us to conceive of morality as style. The relation of Elizabeth Bennet to Darcy is real, is intense, but it expresses itself as a conflict and reconciliation of styles: a formal rhetoric, traditional and rigorous, must find a way to accommodate a female vivacity, which in turn must recognize the principled demands of the strict male syntax. The high moral import of the novel lies in the fact that the union of styles is accomplished without injury to either lover.

Jane Austen knew that *Pride and Prejudice* was a unique success and she triumphed in it. Yet as she listens to her mother reading aloud from the printed book, she becomes conscious of her dissatisfaction with one element of the work. It is the element that is likely to delight us most, the purity and absoluteness of its particular syle.

> The work [she writes in a letter to her sister Cassandra] is rather too light, and bright, and sparkling; it wants to be stretched out here and there with a long chapter of sense, if it could be had; if not, of solemn specious nonsense, about something unconnected with the story; an essay on writing, a critique on Walter Scott, or the history of Buonaparté, or anything that would form a contrast, and bring the reader with increased delight to the playfulness and epigrammatism of the general style.

Her overt concern, of course, is for the increase of the effect of the "general style" itself, which she believes would have been heightened by contrast. But she has in mind something beyond this technical improvement—her sense that the novel is a genre that must not try for the shining outward perfection of style; that it must maintain a degree of roughness of texture, a certain hard literalness; that, for the sake of its moral life, it must violate its own beauty by incorporating some of the irreducible prosy actuality of the world. It is as if she were saying of *Pride and Prejudice* what Henry James says of one of the characters of his story "Crapy Cornelia": "Her grace of ease was perfect, but it was all grace of ease, not a single shred of it grace of uncertainty or of difficulty." [2]

*Mansfield Park,* we may conceive, was the effort to encompass the grace of uncertainty and difficulty. The idea of morality as achieved style, as grace of ease, is not likely ever to be relinquished, not merely because some writers will always assert it anew, but also because morality itself will always insist on it— at a certain point in its development, morality seeks to express its independence of the grinding necessity by which it is engendered, and to claim for itself the autonomy and gratuitousness of art. Yet the idea is one that may easily deteriorate or be perverted. Style, which expresses the innermost truth of any creation or action, can also hide the truth; it is in this sense of the

[2] This may be the place to remark that although the direct line of descent from Jane Austen to Henry James has often been noted, and although there can be no doubt of the lineage, James had a strange misconception of the nature of the art of his ancestress. "Jane Austen, with her light felicity," he says in *The Lesson of Balzac,* "leaves us hardly more curious of her process, or of the experience that fed it, than the brown thrush who tells his story from the garden bough." He says of her reputation that it is higher than her intrinsic interest and attributes it to "the body of publishers, editors, illustrators, producers of the present twaddle of magazines, who have found their 'dear,' our dear, everybody's dear, Jane so infinitely to their material purpose." An acid response to the "dear Jane" myth is always commendable, but it seems to have led James into a strange obtuseness: "The key to Jane Austen's fortune with posterity has been in part the extraordinary grace of her facility, in part of her unconsciousness . . ." This failure of perception (and syntax) is followed by a long, ambiguous, and unfortunate metaphor of Jane Austen musing over her "work-basket, her tapestry flowers, in the spare, cool drawing room of other days." Jane Austen was, it need scarcely be said at this date, as little unconscious as James himself either in her intentions or (as the remarks about the style of *Pride and Prejudice* show) in her "process."

word that we speak of "mere style." *Mansfield Park* proposes to us the possibility of this deception. If we perceive this, we cannot say that the novel is without irony—we must say, indeed, that its irony is more profound than that of any of Jane Austen's other novels. It is an irony directed against irony itself.

In the investigation of the question of character as against personality, of principle as against style and grace of ease as against grace of difficulty, it is an important consideration that the Crawfords are of London. Their manner is the London manner, their style is the *chic* of the metropolis. The city bears the brunt of our modern uneasiness about our life. We think of it as being the scene and the cause of the loss of the simple integrity of the spirit—in our dreams of our right true selves we live in the country. This common mode of criticism of our culture is likely to express not merely our dissatisfaction with our particular cultural situation but our dislike of culture itself, or of any culture that is not a folk culture, that is marked by the conflict of interests and the proliferation and conflict of ideas. Yet the revulsion from the metropolis cannot be regarded merely with skepticism; it plays too large and serious a part in our literature to be thought of as nothing but a sentimentality.

To the style of London Sir Thomas Bertram is the principled antagonist. The real reason for not giving the play, as everyone knows, is that Sir Thomas would not permit it were he at home; everyone knows that a sin is being committed against the absent father. And Sir Thomas, when he returns before his expected time, confirms their consciousness of sin. It is he who identifies the objection to the theatricals as being specifically that of impersonation. His own self is an integer and he instinctively resists the diversification of the self that is implied by the assumption of roles. It is he, in his entire identification with his status and tradition, who makes of Mansfield Park the citadel it is—

it exists to front life and to repel life's mutabilities, like the Peele Castle of Wordsworth's "Elegiac Verses," of which it is said that it is "cased in the unfeeling armor of old time." In this phrase Wordsworth figures in a very precise way the Stoic doctrine of *apatheia,* the principled refusal to experience more emotion than is forced upon one, the rejection of sensibility as a danger to the integrity of the self.

Mansfield stands not only against London but also against what is implied by Portsmouth on Fanny's visit to her family there. Fanny's mother, Lady Bertram's sister, had made an unprosperous marriage, and the Bertrams' minimal effort to assist her with the burdens of a large family had been the occasion of Fanny's coming to live at Mansfield nine years before. Her return to take her place in a home not of actual poverty but of respectable sordidness makes one of the most engaging episodes of the novel, despite our impulse to feel that it ought to seem the most objectionable. We think we ought not be sympathetic with Fanny as, to her slow dismay, she understands that she cannot be happy with her own, her natural, family. She is made miserable by the lack of cleanliness and quiet, of civility and order. We jib at this, we remind ourselves that for the seemliness that does indeed sustain the soul, men too often sell their souls, that warmth and simplicity of feeling may go with indifference to disorder. But if we have the most elementary honesty, we feel with Fanny the genuine pain not merely of the half-clean and the scarcely tidy, of confusion and intrusion, but also of the vulgarity that thrives in these surroundings. It is beyond human ingenuity to define what we mean by vulgarity, but in Jane Austen's novels vulgarity has these elements: smallness of mind, insufficiency of awareness, assertive self-esteem, the wish to devalue, especially to devalue the human worth of other people. That Fanny's family should have forgotten her during her long absence was perhaps inevitable; it is a vulgarity that they have no curiosity about her and no desire to revive the connection, and this indifference is represented as being of a piece with the general indecorum of their lives. We do not blame Fanny when she remembers that in her foster father's house there are many rooms, that hers, although it was small and for years it had been cold, had always been clean and private, that now, although she had once been snubbed and slighted at Mansfield, she is the daughter of Sir Thomas's stern heart.

Of all the fathers of Jane Austen's novels, Sir Thomas is the only one to whom admiration is given. Fanny's real father, Lieutenant Price of the Marines, is shallow and vulgar. The fathers of the heroines of *Pride and Prejudice, Emma,* and *Persuasion,* all lack principle and fortitude; they are corrupted by their belief in their delicate vulnerability—they lack *apatheia.* Yet Sir Thomas is a father, and a father is as little safe from Jane Austen's judgment as he is from Shelley's. Jane Austen's masculine ideal is exemplified by husbands, by Darcy, Knightley, and Wentworth, in whom principle and duty consort with a ready and tender understanding. Sir Thomas's faults are dealt with explicitly—if he learns to cherish Fanny as the daughter of his heart, he betrays the daughters of his blood. Maria's sin and her sister Julia's bad disposition are blamed directly upon his lack of intelligence and sensibility. His principled submission to convention had issued in mere worldliness—he had not seen to it that "principle, active principle" should have its place in the rearing of his daughters, had not given then that "sense of duty which alone can suffice" to govern inclination and temper. He knew of no other way to counteract the low worldly flattery of their Aunt Norris than by the show of that sternness which had alienated them from him. He has allowed Mrs. Norris, the corrupter of his daughters and the persecutor of Fanny, to establish herself in the governance of his home; "she seemed part of himself."

So that Mansfield is governed by an authority all too fallible. Yet Fanny thinks of all that comes "within the view and patronage of Mansfield Park" as "dear to her heart and thoroughly perfect in her eyes." The judgment is not ironical. For the author as well as for the heroine, Mansfield Park is the good place—it is The Great Good Place. It is the house "where all's accustomed, ceremonious," of Yeats's "Prayer for His Daughter"—

> How but in custom and ceremony
> Are innocence and beauty born?

Yet Fanny's loving praise of Mansfield, which makes the novel's last word, does glance at ironies and encompasses ironies. Of these ironies the chief is that Lady Bertram is part of the perfection. All of Mansfield's life makes reference and obeisance to Sir Thomas's wife, who is gentle and without spite, but mindless and moveless, concerned with nothing but the indulgence of her mild, inexorable wants. Middle-aged, stupid, maternal persons are favorite butts for Jane Austen, but although Lady Bertram is teased, she is loved. Sir Thomas's authority must be qualified and tutored by the principled intelligence, the religious intelligence—Fanny's, in effect—but Lady Bertram is permitted to live unregenerate her life of cushioned ease.

I am never quite able to resist the notion that in her attitude to Lady Bertram Jane Austen is teasing herself, that she is turning her irony upon her own fantasy of ideal existence as it presented itself to her at this time. It is scarcely possible to observe how *Mansfield Park* differs from her work that had gone before and from her work that was to come after without supposing that the difference points to a crisis in the author's spiritual life. In that crisis fatigue plays a great part—we are drawn to believe that for the moment she wants to withdraw from the exigent energies of her actual self, that she claims in fancy the right to be rich and fat and smooth and dull like Lady Bertram, to sit on a cushion, to be a creature of habit and an object of ritual deference, not to be conscious, especially not to be conscious of herself. Lady Bertram is, we may imagine, her mocking representation of her wish to escape from the requirements of personality.

It was Jane Austen who first represented the specifically modern personality and the culture in which it had its being. Never before had the moral life been shown as she shows it to be, never before had it been conceived to be so complex and difficult and exhausting. Hegel speaks of the "secularization of spirituality" as a prime characteristic of the modern epoch, and Jane Austen is the first to tell us what this involves. She is the first novelist to represent society, the general culture, as playing a part in the moral life, generating the concepts of "sincerity" and "vulgarity" which no earlier time would have understood the meaning of, and which for us are so subtle that they defy definition, and so powerful that none can escape their sovereignty. She is the first to be aware of the Terror which rules our moral situation, the ubiquitous anonymous judgment to which we respond, the necessity we feel to demonstrate the purity of our secular spirituality, whose dark and dubious places are more numerous and obscure than those of religious spirituality, to put our lives and styles to the question, making sure that not only in deeds but in *décor* they exhibit the signs of our belonging to the number of the secular-spiritual elect.

She herself is an agent of the Terror—we learn from her what our lives should be and by what subtle and fierce criteria they will be judged, and how to pass upon the lives of our friends and fellows. Once we have comprehended her mode of judgment, the moral and spiritual lessons of contemporary literature are easy—the metaphysics of "sincerity" and "vulgarity" once mastered, the modern teachers, Lawrence and Joyce, Yeats and Eliot, Proust and Gide, have but little to add save in the way of contemporary and abstruse examples.

To what extremes the Terror can go she herself has made all too clear in the notorious passage in *Persuasion* in which she comments on Mrs. Musgrove's "large, fat sighings" over her dead scapegrace son. "Personal size and mental sorrow have certainly no necessary proportions," she says. "A large bulky figure has as good a right to be in deep affliction as the most graceful set of limbs in the world. But fair or not fair, there are unbecoming conjunctions, which reason will patronize in vain —which taste cannot tolerate, which ridicule will seize." We feel this to be unconscionable, and Henry James and E. M. Forster will find occasion to warn us that it is one of the signs of the death of the heart to regard a human being as an object of greater or less *vertu;* in fairness to Jane Austen we must remember that the passage occurs in the very novel which deals mercilessly with Sir Walter Elliot for making just this illegitimate application of taste to life. But although this aesthetic-spiritual snobbery is for Jane Austen a unique lapse, it is an extension, an extravagance of her characteristic mode of judgment, and it leads us to see what is implied by the "secularization of spirituality," which requires of us that we judge not merely the moral act itself but also, and even more searchingly, the quality of the agent. This is what Hegel has in mind when he is at such pains to make his distinction between character and personality and to show how the development of the idea of personality is one of the elements of the secularization of spirituality. Dewey followed Hegel in this when, in his *Ethics,* he said that moral choice is not really dictated by the principle or the maxim that is applicable to the situation but rather by the "kind of selfhood" one wishes to "assume." And Nietzsche's conception of the Third Morality, which takes cognizance of the *real*—that is, the unconscious—intention of the agent, is the terrible instrument of criticism of this new development of the moral life. We are likely to feel that this placing of the personality, of the quality of being, at the center of the moral life is a chief glory of spirit in its modern manifestation, and when we take pleasure in Jane Austen we are responding to her primacy and brilliance in the exercise of this new mode of judgment. Yet we at times become aware of the terrible strain it imposes upon us, of the exhausting effort which the concept of personality requires us to make and of the pain of exacerbated sensitivity to others, leading to the *disgust* which is endemic in our culture.

Jane Austen's primacy in representing this mutation in the life of the spirit constitutes a large part of her claim to greatness. But in her representation of the modern situation *Mansfield Park* has a special place. It imagines the self safe from the Terror of secularized spirituality. In the person of Lady Bertram it affirms, with all due irony, the bliss of being able to remain unconscious of the demands of personality (it is a bliss which is a kind of virtue, for one way of being solid, simple, and sincere is to be a vegetable). It shuts out the world and the judgment of the world. The sanctions upon which it relies are not those of culture, of quality of being, of personality, but precisely those which the new conception of the moral life minimizes, the sanctions of principle, and it discovers in principle the path to the wholeness of the self which is peace. When we have exhausted our anger at the offense which *Mansfield Park* offers to our conscious pieties, we find it possible to perceive how intimately it speaks to our secret inexpressible hopes.

# Author's Note

"The Poet as Hero" was written as the introduction to *The Selected Letters of John Keats* (The Great Letters Series, edited by Louis Kronenberger; New York: Farrar, Straus and Young, 1951).

The essay on *"Little Dorrit"* was written as the introduction to the edition of the novel in the New Oxford Illustrated Dickens (London: Geoffrey Cumberlege, Oxford University Press, 1953). It was published in *Kenyon Review*, Autumn, 1953.

The essay on *"Anna Karenina"* was written as the introduction to the Limited Editions Club edition of the novel (Cambridge, England: 1951).

The essay on *The Bostonians* was written as the introduction to the Chiltern Library edition of the novel (London: John Lehmann, 1953).

"Wordsworth and the Rabbis" was read at the celebration of the centenary of Wordsworth's death which was held at Princeton University on April 21 and 22, 1950. It was published, with a different title ("Wordsworth and the Iron Time"), in *Wordsworth: Centenary Studies Presented at Cornell and Princeton Universities,* edited by Gilbert T. Dunklin (Princeton, N.J.: Princeton University Press, 1951). By permission of the Princeton University Press it was also published in *Kenyon Review,* Summer, 1950.

"George Orwell and the Politics of Truth" was written as the introduction to George Orwell's *Homage to Catalonia* (New York: Harcourt, Brace and Company, 1952). It was first published in *Commentary,* March, 1952.

"William Dean Howells and the Roots of Modern Taste" was written as a lecture given at Harvard University in 1951. It was first published in *Partisan Review,* September–October, 1951.

"Flaubert's Last Testament" was written as the introduction to *Bouvard and Pécuchet,* translated by E. W. Stonier and T. W. Earp (Norfolk, Conn.: New Directions, 1954). It was first published in *Partisan Review,* November–December, 1953.

The essay on *"Mansfield Park"* was written as the chapter on Jane Austen for the fifth volume of the *Pelican Guide to English Literature,* edited by Boris Ford. It was first published in *Partisan Review,* September–October, 1954.